EVERYTHING YOU NEED TO KNOW ABOUT
WHEELCHAIR ACCESSIBLE
CRUISING

SYLVIA LONGMIRE

Visit my world at www.spintheglobe.net

First edition published in 2020.

Book design by Sylvia Longmire.

Cover Image: ©Sylvia Longmire

Editing by Erik Deckers

ISBN: 978-1-7345113-0-7

CONTENTS

1 WHY GO ON A CRUISE?

Imagine waking up in the morning, opening the curtains, and watching the sun rise over the walls of a stunning medieval city that you'll be exploring in a few hours. Picture yourself on a gleaming sun deck, reading your favorite book as the ocean breeze blows across your face, occasionally glancing at the turquoise expanse of the Caribbean. Think about what it would be like to have a delicious breakfast in a beautiful dining room in the morning, go whale watching and glacier viewing in the afternoon, and relax with an entertaining theater performance in the evening, all in the same place.

These are just some of the reasons why I personally love cruising, and why I think other travelers should try it if they haven't already. But aside from the scenery and the relaxation that most people associate with cruising, it's logistically one of the easiest ways for wheelchair users to see the world.

Once you board your ship and get settled in your stateroom, you don't have to pack or otherwise move your things until the end of your cruise. You can literally visit half a dozen countries in the span of ten days, yet sleep in the same room and bed every night. And your accessible stateroom is likely to be safer and more compliant with accessibility laws than most hotel rooms—especially in countries outside the United States.

Sometimes, going on a cruise is the only way some wheelchair users can visit certain countries. For example, in August 2017, I spent twelve glorious hours touring St. Petersburg in Russia. It would be extremely difficult for me to fly to St. Petersburg, find a truly accessible hotel room, and explore the city on my own without the availability of accessible taxis or public transportation. (I don't have time or space to discuss the lack of accessibility there in public spaces, buildings, and sidewalks.) However, a local accessible tour company offered a shore excursion for wheelchair users that allowed me to experience a beautiful, if small, piece of Russia that I wouldn't be able to do otherwise.

Much of the magic of cruising occurs on the ship. Food, basic beverages, and entertainment are all included in your fare, and you can do (and eat) as much or as little as you want. I love all the social activities, so you can always find me at trivia, game shows, silent disco, and karaoke. Other cruisers just want to find a quiet corner in the solarium to read a book, or a table in one of the many beautiful lounges or corridors to play cards or mahjong.

Some people have very valid concerns about going on a cruise. Those who are new to cruising or who haven't spent much time on boats might be worried about seasickness. Others don't like the prospect of feeling "trapped" on a ship with no way to get off while at sea. Everyone travels differently, and many people don't like being restricted to a schedule. On most cruises you have the option to eat whenever you want, but you do have to be back on board by a certain time on port days.

Fortunately, there are solutions to most of these concerns. The location of your stateroom on the ship and good medication can really help combat potential seasickness. Some cruise ships are so huge that there's no time to explore all of it, let alone feel confined. Choosing the right cruise line and itinerary can go a long way towards providing you with minimal schedule restrictions outside of boarding requirements.

So, how do you know if a cruise is for you? In the following pages, I will provide a considerable amount of information about wheelchair accessible cruising. First, I'll answer some of the most commonly asked questions about cruises to give you an idea of what it's all about. I'll help you decide which cruise lines might be best for you based on their "personalities," as well as which cruise ships will suit your vacation needs. I'll present some guidelines for choosing the perfect itinerary, and offer an overview of cruising destinations in different parts of the world.

In later chapters, I will cover some important topics, like renting mobility equipment, purchasing travel insurance for your cruise vacation, and cruising tips and things you should know before sailing the high seas. Finally, I have three very important appendices — one with a comprehensive list of tender ports around the world, another with contact information for the accessibility/special needs departments for nine major cruise lines, and another with access and assistance information for Florida cruise ports.

Given that there are twenty-seven global cruise lines operating, over three hundred cruise ships sailing, and even more itineraries and ports of call around the world, it's impossible to go into a significant amount of detail for facilities and operations on specific ships or at specific ports. If I don't answer some of your questions, my recommendation would always be to contact your accessible travel agent or reach out to a cruise line directly for answers. In the meantime, I hope this book provides the information you need to decide that wheelchair accessible cruising is right for you!

2 BEGINNING WITH THE BASICS

What is a tender port? Do I really need to attend a muster drill? Do I have to pay for my food? As an accessible travel agent (someone who specializes in arranging travel for people with accessibility/mobility issues), I get numerous questions from wheelchair users planning for or getting ready to embark on their very first cruise. To familiarize you with what wheelchair accessible cruising is all about, I'll share with you some of the most frequently asked questions I get from my blog readers and clients. Hopefully, these will help you decide if a wheelchair accessible cruise is a good travel option for you.

Are cruise ships wheelchair accessible?

Fortunately, the majority of modern cruise ships that belong to major cruise lines (e.g. Princess, Royal Caribbean, Carnival, Holland America, etc.) are wheelchair accessible. However, the degree of accessibility often varies by the age of the ship. In other words, you have a better chance of good accessibility in staterooms and public areas on a cruise ship that was launched after 2015 then you would for a cruise ship that was launched in the 1990s. Most major cruise lines have tried to adapt older ships as best as possible to be accessible, but you will likely experience more difficulty with them. You will find considerably less accessibility (or none at all) on much smaller cruise ships that are typical for luxury lines like Seabourn, Silversea, Windstar, and Ponant.

Are cruise ship staterooms wheelchair accessible?

On every major cruise line, as noted above, you can find accessible staterooms in almost every category. This means that your stateroom will likely have a wider entryway (usually 32 inches), more room to maneuver in the stateroom, and a bathroom with flat entry, a wider doorway, ideally a roll-under sink, and a roll-in shower with a fold-down bench. Please keep in mind that the specific characteristics of accessible staterooms vary from ship to ship, even within the same cruise line and category. This means that a balcony accessible stateroom on Royal Caribbean's *Oasis of the Seas* will likely look different than an accessible balcony stateroom on Royal Caribbean's *Ovation of the Seas.*

On older cruise ships, there's also a good chance you will have fewer power outlets in your cabin, and usually they will be located by the desk and not next to your bed. You may need to ask for an extension cord or bring your own if you have many electronics or medical devices that you need to charge. Space in a cabin, particularly around the bed, will vary from ship to ship, as will the ease or difficulty with which you can access the balcony. The size and comfort of fold-down benches in the accessible shower will vary. If you have very specific needs with regards to your stateroom, it's best to contact the accessibility department (see Appendix B) directly for the cruise line you're interested in sailing with.

Can I use a power wheelchair or electric scooter on the ship?

If you will be cruising on a larger cruise ship, typically with 750 or more passengers, then you should have no trouble using a power wheelchair or electric scooter. Please keep in mind that you have to store them inside your stateroom, and they can never be left parked in the hallway for safety reasons. Always check with the cruise line or your accessible travel agent before booking to ensure that your particular mobility aid will fit in your stateroom. If you have not booked an accessible stateroom, please keep in mind that the width of a regular stateroom doorway is typically 22 inches. Most wheelchairs and scooters will not fit through the doorway of a regular stateroom.

Will I be able to get off the ship at every port?

If your itinerary includes a tender-only port, this means that passengers have to get shuttled from the cruise ship to the port dock on the lifeboats, which are used as tender vessels. In most cases, wheelchair users will not be allowed to board tender vessels. However, there are some exceptions. Most Holland America ships have accessible tendering platforms; so does the Celebrity *Edge* and some Norwegian Cruise Lines ships. Manual wheelchair users will have a much easier time getting permission to tender, especially if the wheelchair user can walk a few steps onto the tender boat and carry a folding wheelchair with them.

Ultimately, the decision to allow anyone to tender, including wheelchair users, is at the discretion of the captain, and may be prohibited due to tidal conditions or the weather. While there should generally be no issues with wheelchair users disembarking at docked ports, please keep in mind that tidal conditions can affect the steepness of the gangways. The crew is trained to help wheelchair users board and disembark at ports of call.

Are meals included in the cruise price?

The short answer is, yes. All meals in the formal dining rooms are included, as well as some casual dining options on certain ships, like pizza, hamburgers, ice cream, etc. Some cruise ships have smaller cafés with free sandwiches, cookies, and dessert options. Almost all cruise ships also have buffet restaurants that are open during various hours, and all of that food is also included in your cruise price. What is not included are specialty dining restaurants that tend to have themes like steakhouses, seafood, Asian or Italian dining, etc. The fee for eating at these restaurants can range anywhere from $25-$55 per person per dining experience depending on the cruise line. Some cruise lines also have exclusive restaurants with access available only to passengers who book staterooms in higher-end suite categories.

Are sodas and alcoholic beverages included in the cruise price?

Usually they're not, although different cruise lines run sales at different times of the year that do include free beverage packages as a "perk." Typically, you can drink regular coffee, tea, lemonade, and juice at no extra charge. However, if you prefer to drink soda, bottled water, specialty coffees, or alcoholic beverages, you will need to purchase a beverage package or pay for the beverage with your cruise card when you order it. Depending on the cruise line, beverage packages can vary in price from approximately $29-$59 per person per day.

Do the swimming pools on cruise ships have lifts?

Some do and some don't. You are more likely to find a swimming pool lift on newer cruise ships. A few older ones have retrofitted them, but they are not as common on ships launched prior to 2010. A few cruise ships have the pool lift permanently in place. However, others bring them out and install them by request only to prevent children and other passengers from playing with them or using them inappropriately. If swimming in the pool is a priority for you, please check with the cruise line or your accessible travel agent to confirm that the ship you would like to sail on has a pool lift available.

Will my cell phone work on the ship?

No, in the sense that you can't access a cellular network at sea. However, if you have an international calling plan, which you need to set up at an additional charge through your cell phone carrier, you may be able to use your cell phone at the ports of call. Technically, there is a service called Cellular at Sea that some ships have available, and will allow you to make cellular phone calls from the ship. However, the charge for this is usually $4.99 a minute.

Is there Wi-Fi Internet available on cruise ships?

Yes, but it will cost you, unless you book a cruise with a sale that includes a Wi-Fi package. Most cruises allow you to book Internet packages that include a certain number of minutes, and the cost varies from cruise line to cruise line. For example, Princess offers packages from sixty minutes for $49 to six hundred minutes for $199. Other lines offer unlimited Internet access packages that vary in price depending on the length of the cruise. Keep an eye out for cruise line sales that offer perks, as free Wi-Fi is often one of the perks being offered. The speed is typically much slower than you will find on land, but it's your only option if you really need Internet access while you're at sea.

Do cruise lines offer accessible shore excursions?

Sometimes, and when they do, the options often aren't all that great. I've had the best luck with accessible shore excursion options with Princess and Royal Caribbean. If you do find an accessible shore excursion through the cruise line, often it's just a windshield tour. This means you're on a bus or minivan with a lift, and taking a scenic tour of your port of call with only one or two stops for pictures. However, I have taken some pretty amazing accessible shore excursions booked through the cruise line. It just all depends on the itinerary and availability of accessible transportation at your ports of call.

If you book your cruise through an **accessible travel agent**, which I highly recommend, he or she can help you arrange independent shore excursions with local accessible tour companies. Private tours will almost always cost you more money, but generally offer more flexibility and options for sightseeing then something booked through the ship. Shore excursions can cost anywhere from $39 per person for a large group tour to $750 per person for a private tour, so it really depends on what's available at each port of call and what type of activity you're interested in.

Can I participate in activities on board the ship?

Absolutely. I go on cruises several times a year, and I try to participate in as many social activities, trivia games, and game shows as possible. Cruise lines have worked to make their public areas as wheelchair accessible as possible, and their social activities as inclusive as possible. On older ships, some of the public spaces are unfortunately only accessible by stairs. However, newer ships have dance floors, plazas/atriums, and lounge floors with flat entry. Even for karaoke, they will adjust the screen and microphone to a place you can access.

Are theaters and other live entertainment venues accessible?

Yes. Every main theater where the big production shows take place has designated wheelchair seating. However, depending on the theater layout and the age of the ship, the view may be wonderful or may not be that great. Newer ships tend to have reserved seating at the top of the lower level and the balcony level, and usually at the bottom of the lower level accessible by elevator or lift. Older ships may only have reserved seating at the top/back of the theater, and possibly with obstructed views. Smaller lounges with pianos or acoustic entertainment are accessible, but space can get tight if it contains larger chairs and lots of people. You may have to ask people to move out of your way to maneuver in between chairs.

Can I rent medical equipment or mobility aids for use on my cruise?

Yes, and usually you can have it delivered directly to your stateroom on the ship. However, please keep in mind that the availability of these items varies depending on your port of departure. Almost always you can rent a scooter or manual wheelchair, but the availability for hospital beds, hoists, and other heavier or more specialized equipment may be limited. You can read much more about this in Chapter 13.

Should I purchase a trip protection plan?

Absolutely, without a doubt. If you are cruising to another country, your medical insurance in your home country will not cover you if you get sick or injured while traveling. If you have to go to an emergency room or get medically evacuated, those bills can start tallying into the thousands or tens of thousands of dollars. Depending on the country, you may have to either pay in cash upfront before receiving medical care or show proof that you can afford to pay for your medical care.

If you have a travel insurance policy, you will get reimbursed for eligible expenses up to the limit of your policy. Especially if you have a disability or pre-existing medical conditions, purchasing a trip protection plan is essential. You can read more about travel insurance in Chapter 14.

How much do cruises typically cost?

There are several factors that go into determining the cost of going on a cruise. The first is the duration of the cruise. A three-night cruise will almost always be cheaper than a seven-night cruise. The second is the type of stateroom you prefer. Interior or inside staterooms, which have no windows, are always the least expensive. Prices go up incrementally for oceanview staterooms, which have just a window, then balcony staterooms, then suites.

The third is the cruise line. Carnival, for example, is considered a budget cruise line and usually has the least expensive itineraries. Moderate budget cruise lines include Norwegian and Royal Caribbean, premium includes Princess and Holland America, and the luxury would include Celebrity, Disney, Cunard, and Azamara. Fourth is the itinerary. Caribbean cruises tend to be the least expensive, while Mediterranean and Asian itineraries will be more expensive. South America and Antarctic itineraries tend to be some of the most expensive.

Fifth is the time of year. High season (i.e. the most expensive) for European and Alaska itineraries is the middle of summer, and for Caribbean cruises the high season is usually when children are out of school. Sailings during American holidays are almost always more expensive. To give you some ballpark figures, for a three-night Carnival cruise from a Florida port to the Bahamas, you can expect to pay approximately $450 per person for an inside cabin. For a seven-day Alaska inside passage cruise in a balcony stateroom on Princess, you can expect to pay approximately $1,600 per person.

Do I need a passport to go on a cruise?

This depends on the cruise itinerary. If you're a US citizen and are going on a closed-loop (i.e. round-trip) itinerary from a US port, generally you will only need a birth certificate and a form of identification. However, even on a closed-loop cruise, some countries on your itinerary may insist on examining your passport. Your cruise line or travel agent can tell you what the passport and visa requirements are for your cruise. Regardless of the itinerary, I tell all of my clients to bring a passport. If an emergency occurs while you're ashore at a foreign port of call, you will have a much harder time getting home without a passport.

3 CRUISE SHIP 101

What's the difference between port and starboard? What kind of stateroom should I book? What activities are available for my kids? How do I find my way around? Now that you know some basic information about cruising, you may want to know what to expect when you actually board a cruise ship. These are common questions many first-time cruisers have about the ship itself. While no two cruise ships are identical, the basics are similar enough that I can provide you with a basic overview of what to expect before you set sail.

Basic cruise ship layout

Modern cruise ships come in many different shapes, sizes, and colors. They can carry as few hundred passengers or as many as six thousand. However, the fundamentals of cruise ship construction and layout are pretty similar from ship to ship.

The number will depend on the size of the ship, but you will have several different decks, or levels. The typical cruise ships I write about in this book belong to major cruise lines, and carry no fewer than two thousand passengers. As such, the cruise ships you are most likely to sail on will have anywhere from ten to twenty decks. Almost every deck will have passenger staterooms, but a few will have none.

Starting from the bottom of the cruise ship and working your way up, the lowest deck is for tendering, sometimes for disembarking at ports of call, and the medical center. The next decks up (usually Deck 2 or 3) will usually be only for staterooms. Deck 4 or Deck 5 will be the main embarkation level, where you can find guest services, the shore excursions desk, the purser, the bottom level of the ship's atrium or plaza, and some bars and lounges. On this deck, you may also find an art gallery and a photography studio. A main dining room will likely be on this level in the aft section, and the lower level of the theater will likely be in the forward section.

The next deck up (and possibly one more on a larger ship) is likely a promenade-style deck. Here is where you will find lounges, bars, shops, and the casino. You may also find a second level for the main dining room and the theater, and perhaps different specialty restaurants. The decks between this one and the pool deck will likely be only for passenger staterooms.

The pool deck is one of the uppermost decks on the ship. It will sometimes have a large screen for showing poolside movies, and a stage for entertainment. Exercise classes are also usually held on the pool deck, as well as different games and contests. Most cruise ships have several bars and smaller casual eateries around or near the pool. This is usually the deck where you will also find the buffet.

Above the pool deck is typically a sun deck, which has plenty of lounge chairs and possibly a jogging track. Many sun decks have bars, and depending on the cruise ship, this might be where waterslides are located. Any decks located higher up may not have elevator access. This is where you will find sports courts for activities like basketball, and more lounge chairs. The highest indoor/outdoor deck with elevator access will commonly have a large observation lounge that becomes a nightclub in the later hours.

Accessible staterooms

While the size, quality, and amenities in cruise ship staterooms vary widely between cruise lines, and often between ships within the same cruise line, there are several common stateroom categories. Each primary stateroom category has an accessible version.

The main difference is that accessible staterooms are larger than the non-accessible equivalent, have wider doorways, flat entry to the bathroom, roll-in showers with grab bars, and either ramped or flat access to balconies. Many accessible staterooms also have emergency pull cords and call buttons.

Interior – This is the smallest and the least expensive type of cruise ship stateroom. They are located in the interior portion of most passenger decks, and as such, have no windows. Depending on the ship, interior staterooms can accommodate from two to four passengers.

Oceanview – These staterooms are the next step up from the interior category, and are located along the exterior of the ship. They either have a porthole or a picture window that varies in size from ship to ship. Depending on the ship, oceanview staterooms can accommodate from two to four passengers.

Balcony/Veranda – These staterooms are larger than oceanview cabins, and have either a glass hinged door or a sliding door that leads to a balcony. Balconies vary in size from ship to ship. Balcony wheelchair access also varies, with some ships having a smooth threshold, and others requiring a portable ramp and considerable effort to get over the sliding glass door track. Depending on the ship, balcony staterooms can accommodate from two to four passengers.

Suite – Suites are the largest and most expensive staterooms on a cruise ship, and have several subcategories varying in size and price. Some ships have junior suites, which are larger than a regular balcony stateroom, but smaller and less expensive than a deluxe suite with more amenities. Depending on the ship, suites can accommodate from two to four passengers, and sometimes more depending on the suite category.

There is also a wide variety of bedding configurations. Staterooms designed for double occupancy will have either a king bed or a queen bed that can be separated into two twin beds upon request. Staterooms that can accommodate three or more people will either have a double sofa bed, bunk beds that pull down from the ceiling, or Murphy style beds that pull down from the wall.

Please keep in mind that accessing the pull-down bunk beds requires the use of a lightweight and narrow ladder. This may pose a challenge for some passengers. Depending on the configuration of the stateroom, wheelchair users may not be able to access certain parts of the stateroom when all of the beds are pulled open.

NOTE: Some cruise ships have smaller (and cheaper) solo staterooms for passengers traveling alone. However, there are currently no wheelchair accessible solo staterooms on any cruise line.

Food and beverage

Cruises are notorious for helping passengers pack on the pounds, and it's absolutely true that you have a wide variety of dining options on cruise ships. This is because cruise lines know that people have a wide variety of dining preferences.

The first dining option for passengers is the main dining room, also known as the MDR. This is a more formal setting with linen tablecloths and silverware, although you don't necessarily have to dress up to eat in the MDR (aside from covering your swimsuit and wearing shoes). You will be presented with a menu, and most ships have food items that vary from night to night, as well as a "classic" food selection that always stays the same. You can eat breakfast and dinner in the MDR during specific times.

The next option is the buffet. Contrary to popular belief, cruise ship buffets do close most sections for brief periods of time during the day to get ready for the next meal. For many cruise lines, the midnight buffet is a thing of the past, although the buffet usually has some basic food offerings like pizza or sandwiches throughout the night. Cruise ship buffets offer an incredible variety of food, including salads, fruits, breads and cheeses, entrées from around the world, burgers and pizza, and desserts.

Many cruise ships offer more casual dining options located around the ship. Some of these eateries offer food that is included in your cruise fare, and others charge an extra fee. Almost every cruise ship has café that offers premium cappuccinos, lattes, and other specialty coffees, along with premium desserts and bakery items. Some ships have burger and pizza eateries, taco bars and Mexican themed eateries, and ice cream or gelato counters.

If you plan on drinking anything other than tap water, iced tea, juice, or basic coffee, you will have to spend money. You can purchase other beverages, such as soda or alcohol, as you go or purchase a specialty drink package. Lower-cost packages will include bottled water, sodas, and specialty coffees, while higher-end packages will include beer, wine, and liquor. Beverage package prices vary from cruise line to cruise line, and are often included as a free "perk" during sale periods.

Entertainment

One of the fun things about cruising is that there's always something going on! Each night, your cabin steward will provide you with a schedule of events for the following day. Alternatively, you can view the schedule for each day on the cruise line's phone app for your ship. Entertainment usually include live music, ranging from acoustic duos to full-on stage productions in the main theater. Many cruise ships have a house band that performs once or twice each night in one of the lounges. The type of music tends to vary based on the average age of the ship's clientele.

The cruise director and his or her staff are responsible for all the social events during your cruise. These can include trivia, which usually happens two or three times a day, game shows, and competitions like paper plane throwing or Nerf archery. During the cruise, there will also be larger events like sail-away parties, late night theme parties with dance music around the pool, silent disco parties, and even singing competitions.

Pools and hot tubs

Every cruise ship has at least one pool, and usually at least one hot tub. They're filled with salt water, and are typically quite small. Unfortunately, it can be challenging to find a pool lift on a cruise ship. You will have much better luck with newer and larger ships in this regard. Some cruise ships have lifts for their hot tubs as well. However, finding a lift for a secondary or solarium pool on many ships is hit or miss.

Please note that maneuvering in the pool area while the ship is at sea can be challenging because it gets very crowded. Some ships arrange their lounge chairs more efficiently to allow space for both walkers and non-walkers alike, and some don't. Fortunately, passengers are generally very kind and considerate if you have to ask them to move their lounge chairs so you can get by.

Kids programs

Technically, every major cruise line has a kids program on their cruise ships. However, the quality and variety of activities tends to vary based on the cruise line demographic. For example, Disney Cruise Line has the best kids program at sea, hands-down. Their entire cruise line exists to serve families with children, so this should come as no surprise. Royal Caribbean and Carnival also have great kids programs because they welcome tons of families on their cruise ships, especially in the Caribbean and during the summer.

This isn't to say that kids programs on other cruise lines aren't good; it's just that they may not have many kids on their ships because of the itinerary or the target demographic. For example, I've never seen more than a handful of children on a Celebrity cruise, and there were maybe four on my Princess Alaska cruise in May (before summer break). I can't imagine young children having a great time on a Cunard transatlantic sailing, or some older Holland America ships on a Southeast Asia itinerary.

Medical services

Every cruise ship for the major lines has an infirmary with staff available twenty-four hours a day to care for passengers. However, these facilities are typically equipped to treat only minor non-emergency conditions. If you develop a serious illness or a major emergency condition, you will either be referred to a medical facility at the next port of call, or in a serious emergency, evacuated by helicopter from the cruise ship.

Smaller ships typically have one doctor and two nurses on board, and larger cruise ships often have two doctors with three or four nurses. This staff must be able to perform advanced life support practices, emergency cardiovascular care, and minor surgical procedures. They're expected to stabilize seriously ill patients, perform reasonable diagnostic and therapeutic interventions, and help evacuate seriously sick or injured patients. The infirmary will have regular hours for minor illnesses, but will also have staff on call twenty-four hours a day for emergencies.

In case your malady requires medication, pharmacy stocks are available on board, which means you will have access to basic medicines. The size of the inventory varies by ship, but staff will be able to provide you with antibiotics, seasickness pills, aspirin, and other common medicines. You will have to pay for onboard medical care and any prescriptions out of pocket. However, your travel insurance policy will reimburse you once you file a claim at the end of your cruise.

4 SELECTING A CRUISE LINE

Every cruise line has its own personality. That's a very simplified way of saying that each cruise line markets and caters to a particular demographic. That's not to say that the same person can't sail on very different cruise lines and have a great vacation each time. It's just important for you, in my opinion, to understand what that target demographic is — or personality — for each cruise line so you can make decisions about which one to use based on what you're looking for in an accessible cruise.

There are more than two dozen cruise lines in operation right now. Some own the "mega ships" that carry thousands of passengers, and some are more boutique in nature, with small or expedition-style ships. In this chapter, I will only cover the major cruise lines that have ships with an appreciable amount of accessible features.

Carnival

Carnival is the largest cruise conglomerate in the world, and is the original "fun ship" line (if you remember those Kathy Gifford commercials). Carnival is also what you would call a budget cruise line. It caters largely to families, people looking to spend the least amount of money for a cruise vacation, and large groups looking to drink and have a lot of boisterous fun. Carnival ships are where you'll find family reunions with members all wearing the same T-shirt. Food quality varies from ship to ship, the décor in staterooms is very plain and basic, and the décor in public areas tends to be extremely bright and colorful.

Carnival has really good kids programs, with characters like Dr. Seuss embedded in their activities. Accessible features in older ships are sometimes lacking, especially if they haven't been refurbished in several years, but they're excellent in newer ships. Carnival does offer accessible shore excursions at some ports of call. (I have personally sailed with Carnival.)

Celebrity

Celebrity is part of the Royal Caribbean Cruise Lines family, and is one of their luxury brands. Most of their ships and itineraries, and the company as a whole, tend to appeal to an older crowd. While you will still find many couples in their thirties and forties on Celebrity cruises, the average age on many ships tends to be around sixty. You will find very few families with children on Celebrity cruises. Celebrity offers itineraries around the world, but really shines with itineraries between ten to sixteen nights. Their cruises tend to be on the pricier side, especially for sailings the Celebrity *Edge*, their newest ship. The *Apex*, which is the *Edge*'s sister ship, will debut in April 2020, and will likely have more expensive itineraries as well. However, you get what you pay for. The food is excellent on Celebrity ships, as is the service and the cleanliness. Partly because of the older demographic, the accessibility on Celebrity ships is outstanding, which is why it's my favorite cruise line. Celebrity does offer accessible shore excursions at some ports of call. (I have personally sailed with Celebrity.)

Cunard

Cunard is a cruise line that has been around for some time, dating back to the early 1800s. The *Lusitania*, which was sunk in 1915 and led to Britain's involvement in World War I, was actually a Cunard ship. The UK-based line only operates three ships: *Queen Victoria*, *Queen Elizabeth*, and *Queen Mary II*. It is probably best known for its transatlantic voyages, and longer itineraries that include around-the-world cruises. The demographic skews much older, with the average age around seventy. Cunard is considered a luxury brand, and cruises can be on the expensive side. The décor is extremely traditional, and dinner is often a dressy affair, with several gala nights on each cruise. The programming is very low-key, and the onboard atmosphere subdued. It is rare to find children on a Cunard cruise. Because I have not personally sailed with Cunard, I am not aware of their accessible shore excursion offerings.

Disney

Disney has absolutely translated anything and everything related to the theme parks to their cruise line. The service, the food, the décor, and the shows are absolutely top-notch across the board. Their kids program is the best in the industry. The demographic is obviously families, but you will find many Disney fans with no children cruising on their ships. Disney currently has four ships: *Fantasy*, *Wonder*, *Magic*, and *Dream*. They offer more variety of itineraries in the Caribbean and Alaska, but have very limited offerings in Hawaii, Mexico, the Pacific Coast, and Europe. The wheelchair accessibility is absolutely outstanding. Disney is one of the few cruise lines that offer accessible family staterooms (which aren't technically suites, although they do offer those) with berths for more than four people.

Because you get what you pay for, Disney is easily one of the most expensive major cruise lines in the industry. However, they will try to provide you with almost anything you could possibly ask for, especially with regard to accessibility. Disney does offer accessible shore excursions at some ports of call. (I have personally sailed with Disney.)

Holland America

Affectionately known as HAL in the cruise industry, Holland America is one of the oldest cruise lines still sailing. It is considered a luxury brand, and that is reflected everywhere on its ships, from the décor to the food. HAL offers itineraries all over the world, specializing in longer itineraries over two weeks and up to several months for its around-the-world cruises. HAL is also well-known for its Alaska itineraries. The cruise line has partnered with Oprah Winfrey and America's Test Kitchen for onboard experiences, and the food is truly outstanding.

The demographic is considerably older, with the average age between sixty and seventy. The atmosphere on many of its ships, as such, is very mellow with low-key programming on days at sea and in the evenings. People tend to dress more elegantly for dinners and the buffet closes at 8:30 PM on some ships. Because of the older demographic, accessibility tends to be outstanding. Holland America does offer accessible shore excursions at some ports of call. (I have personally sailed with Holland America.)

MSC

MSC is a lower budget cruise line based out of Italy. Their itineraries are mostly in Europe, but they do offer Caribbean itineraries on a few ships out of Miami. The demographic is quite broad, with many families on their Caribbean cruises. The décor is extremely modern, with many mirrors and bright lights, akin to a night club. Passengers tend to be mostly European, with very few English speakers on their European cruises. Announcements are made in multiple languages, even out of Miami, and English is not the primary language on board except for game shows and theater performances. Most crew members, however, speak English.

Food quality is average, as is the service. However, their kids program is quite good. Accessibility on their newest ships is above average, but there are no automatically opening doors anywhere on board. MSC does offer accessible shore excursions at some ports of call. However, they are subject to cancellation if not enough people sign up for them. (I have personally sailed with MSC.)

Norwegian (NCL)

Like Carnival, Norwegian is also considered a lower budget cruise line, but is a step above Carnival with regards to service, food quality, and décor, in my opinion. Norwegian has itineraries all around the world, and will often be seen docking right next door to luxury cruise liners. Itineraries vary typically from three nights to seven nights. Their demographic is pretty broad, and certainly attract families with children, especially on Caribbean itineraries throughout the year. The food is pretty good, and the specialty restaurants are actually quite affordable. Norwegian also has a good kids' program. Accessibility is very good on Norwegian ships, especially the newer ones. Some Norwegian ships also have the ability to board wheelchair users onto tender boats. Norwegian does offer accessible shore excursions at some ports of call. (I have personally sailed with Norwegian.)

Princess

Princess is another cruise line that has been around for many years, and is the original "Love Boat." It's considered a higher-end cruise line the Royal Caribbean, but not quite as luxury minded as Celebrity or perhaps Holland America. Princess offers itineraries all over the world, and is probably best known for its outstanding Alaska cruises. The demographic tends to skew older, especially for Alaska, Panama Canal, and Europe itineraries, and their kids' programs are not very robust. The food is generally excellent, and so is the service.

The quality of the ships varies widely. Their older ships that haven't been refurbished in a few years are definitely lacking in public area accessibility, with many heavy wooden doors and no automatically opening doors. The décor and cleanliness of the staterooms, especially the bathrooms, varies depending on the age of the ship. Newer Princess ships will have much better accessibility. Princess does offer accessible shore excursions at some ports of call. (I have personally sailed with Princess.)

Royal Caribbean

Like its competitor Carnival, Royal Caribbean has one of the largest fleets of cruise ships in the world. They offer itineraries everywhere, from three nights to the Bahamas to seven nights and longer in other parts of the world. Older ships in the fleet tend to be smaller, carrying around 2,500 passengers. However, their Oasis class has the largest cruise ship currently in the market — the Symphony of the Seas, which carries over 6,600 passengers at capacity. You will find passengers from all demographic groups on Royal Caribbean cruises. Part of it depends on the itinerary. On Alaska cruises, you'll find mostly older couples, with some families during June and July. There are several families with children on their Caribbean itineraries throughout the year, and their European itineraries are mixed depending on the month. In my opinion, their kids' program is second only to Disney Cruise Lines.

Royal Caribbean is considered a mid-priced cruise line, with nicely appointed ships and comfortable staterooms. The accessibility overall is excellent, and is particularly outstanding on their Oasis class ships.

Royal Caribbean does offer accessible shore excursions at some ports of call. (I have personally sailed with Royal Caribbean.)

This is far from an exhaustive list of all the cruise lines currently operating. While there are other cruise lines that do offer accessible staterooms and would be suitable for many wheelchair users, these are the major lines sailing from ports in United States that offer at least decent wheelchair accessibility. Other smaller cruise lines that you may want to investigate on your own include Azamara (luxury, smaller ships), P&O (lower budget, UK-based), and Oceania (higher-budget, smaller ships).

5 SELECTING A CRUISE SHIP

As an accessible travel agent and frequent cruiser, one of the questions I get asked the most is, *What is the most accessible cruise ship out there?* The great news is that wheelchair users have more and more options for great accessibility on cruise ships every year. While I haven't been on every single cruise ship sailing the oceans today, I have a really good idea of what wheelchair users should look for and ask about when trying to determine the accessibility of a cruise ship they would like to sail on.

Age Before Beauty

There are some absolutely stunning cruise ships out there right now, and they can rival any five-star hotel on land. But, just because the ship is luxurious and beautiful doesn't mean that it's wheelchair friendly. One of the better indicators of wheelchair accessibility on a cruise ship is its age. It's incredibly difficult to retrofit an older cruise ship to include accessibility features. However, with an average of eight brand-new cruise ships launching every year, it's becoming easier for ship architects and designers to incorporate accessibility features from the start. To find out the age of the ship, you can either Google the ship's name or find its fact sheet on the cruise line website. You'll also be able to find out when the ship had its most recent dry-dock renovation or retrofit.

Staterooms: Bigger is Always Better

Many people who have never cruised before are shocked at how small cruise ship cabins can be. Fortunately, accessible cabins are bigger by necessity because wheelchair users need enough space to maneuver around beds, and into and out of the bathroom. That being said, the actual size of a cruise ship accessible cabin can vary widely between cruise lines, and even ships in the same class within a cruise line. An interior stateroom will be the smallest category, and you shouldn't accept anything smaller than two hundred square feet for an accessible cabin that can accommodate two people, one of whom is in a wheelchair.

Take note that some cruise lines offer different types of accessible staterooms. "Fully accessible" means that you can access both sides of the bed. "Single-side approach" means that the bed is pushed up against the wall, so you can only get into it from one side. "Ambulatory accessible" means the cabin is designed for someone with mobility limitations, but who doesn't use a wheelchair or scooter. These rooms will still have accessible bathrooms with roll-in showers.

All Ship Showers are Not Created Equal

One of the biggest problems I have with roll-in showers on cruise ships is that many of them have itty-bitty fold down seats with vinyl straps. I am a very thin person, and even I find these small square seats to be uncomfortable and not particularly safe. I much prefer cruise ships with roll-in showers that have wide laminated wood fold-down benches. They may be a little more uncomfortable to sit on, but it gives me much more room to transfer and maneuver. They also tend to be less slippery. Sometimes it can be hard to find out what type of seating is available in accessible cabin showers, but a quick Google search for your cruise ship and the phrase "accessible cabin" should turn up at least one photo or video. If worse comes to worst, you can call the cruise line's accessibility department and ask.

Asking for a Lift

Fortunately for wheelchair users, the newest and largest cruise ships have lifts that allow wheelchair users to get into the ship's pool. Most of them are portable, and sometimes cruise lines will ask you to provide several hours' notice before going to the pool so that the crew can install it for you. This was the case on the *Disney Dream* when I sailed on it in July 2018. However, both the *Harmony of the Seas* and the *Allure of the Seas* (Royal Caribbean) had pool lifts that were permanently installed. If the ability to swim in the ship's pool is very important to you, your travel agent can find out if your ship has a lift, or you can call the cruise line's accessibility department. Special Needs at Sea also maintains a list of cruise ship accessibility features that indicates if pool lifts are available.

Shore Excursion Options

I'm extremely excited to see that with every cruise I take, more and more cruise lines are offering accessible shore excursions. The options are generally not many, and they aren't always exciting. However, they are much less expensive than independently booking a private accessible tour with a local supplier. You can do a search online within a ship's itinerary to see what shore excursions are available, and filter them to see if any are accessible. Please keep in mind that sometimes accessible shore excursion options pop up closer to the cruise departure date, and sometimes after you depart.

Out in Public

Determining the wheelchair accessibility of public areas on a specific cruise ship can be difficult prior to embarkation. However, more and more people are creating video tours of cruise ships and posting them on YouTube. This has been really helpful for me when trying to determine if I will be cramped for space in a dining room or poolside or in a lounge. Almost all modern cruise ships have reserved seating in their primary theater for wheelchair users, but it's not always great. On older ships, sometimes the view is obstructed by a huge pole, or because the reserved seats are at the top of the lower level, sometimes the top half of the stage background is cut off by the edge of the balcony above.

Some main dining rooms have more space than others, but the crew is generally really good about moving chairs out of your way so you can reach your table, and removing any chairs you might need in order to sit at the table. For these sorts of things, it can be helpful to join a social media group for wheelchair travelers and ask members if they have cruised on that specific ship.

As you can see, there are many different factors that go into making a cruise ship as accessible as possible for wheelchair users. But none of these things are any good if the ship's crew doesn't have the right attitude towards passengers with disabilities. Based on my extensive cruising experience as a wheelchair user, here are my favorite accessible cruise ships.

Celebrity Edge

I got the first hint that the brand-new Celebrity *Edge* wasn't going to be the typical cruise ship the second I rolled on board. I felt like I had just entered the lobby of a W Hotel filled with famous and important people I hadn't seen on TV yet. Subtle dance club music was playing at a volume loud enough to energize you, but low enough where you could converse normally. There was glass and metal and sleek wood and modernity everywhere. It's Celebrity's newest ship, launched at the very end of 2018, and it was built with accessibility in mind. I know, because Celebrity executives and designers consulted with me on a couple of those aspects. The wheelchair accessibility on the Celebrity *Edge* was superb; better than any cruise ship I've been on.

Celebrity offers accessible shore excursions at many ports of call. But what's truly unique about this ship is the Magic Carpet accessible tendering system that allows wheelchair users to get off the ship at tender ports (given good conditions). Celebrity is launching the *Edge*'s sister ship *Apex* in April 2020, and you can expect it to have similar accessibility features.

The Stats: Twenty-five accessible staterooms, no-threshold bathrooms and balconies, roll-in showers with fold-down benches, grab bars, lowered roll-under sinks, open bed frames, lifts at main pool and whirlpool, lowered casino tables, accessible tendering system, reserved wheelchair seating in theater.

Royal Caribbean Oasis Class

This is Royal Caribbean's newest class of ships, and includes the (currently) largest cruise ship in the world. These sister ships – *Symphony of the Seas, Harmony of the Seas, Oasis of the Seas,* and *Allure of the Seas* – have all been launched within the last decade, with the *Harmony* (2016) and *Symphony* (2018) being the newest (and biggest). The *Symphony* is a leviathan, with a capacity of over six thousand passengers. Royal Caribbean has repeatedly demonstrated a commitment to accessibility on its ships, both in new construction and during dry-dock renovations. The accessible cabins on these ships are the largest I've ever seen, and Royal Caribbean offers more accessible shore excursions than most cruise lines.

I recently cruised on the older *Mariner of the Seas,* which was launched in 2003 and most recently refurbished in 2018. Royal Caribbean modified it to include many features similar to the Oasis class ships, like the Promenade area and some of the eateries like Johnny Rockets. I loved that all the doorways between indoor and outdoor areas, except for one, had sliding glass doors. So basically, while the Oasis class has the best accessibility due to being newer, don't automatically discount older Royal Caribbean ships.

The Stats: Forty-six accessible staterooms, no-threshold bathrooms and balconies, roll-in showers with fold-down benches, grab bars, lowered roll-under sinks, open bed frames, lowered closet rods, lifts at main pool and whirlpool, lowered casino tables, lowered bar counters, reserved wheelchair seating in main theater, Aqua Theater, and Studio B.

Disney Dream

When most people think of Disney, they think of first-class service, and their cruise ships are no exception. Disney Cruise Lines is serious about inclusion and understands that wheelchair users have families, too. I sailed on the *Dream* in July 2018 with my two children and my parents in an accessible family stateroom, and I was just so thrilled to see that Disney ships offer accessible staterooms for families larger than four people. They even offer special equipment for the staterooms, like bed rails and transfer benches. The accessibility of all the dining rooms and public areas was impeccable, as was the customer service and crew attitude.

I didn't book any accessible shore excursions through Disney because we had independent arrangements in Nassau. While my boys didn't disembark at Castaway Cay, I was able to see the fantastic wheelchair accessibility there for myself.

The Stats: Twenty-five accessible staterooms, no-threshold bathrooms and balconies, roll-in showers with fold-down benches, grab bars, lowered roll-under sinks, open bed frames, lowered closet bars, lift at main pool (upon request with advance notice), reserved wheelchair seating in main theater. The Disney *Fantasy* (launched in 2012) is the *Dream*'s sister ship, so you can expect to find the same accessibility features.

Celebrity Solstice Class

I first began my love affair with Celebrity when I sailed on the *Silhouette* for twelve nights from Rome in November 2017. My best friend and I visited multiple ports of call in Greece and Israel, and I distinctly remember thinking repeatedly that the ship felt like it was designed for wheelchair users. The *Silhouette* (2011) is a Solstice-class ship, and her sisters include the Celebrity *Solstice* (2008), *Equinox* (2009), *Eclipse* (2010), and *Reflection* (2012). I had an accessible interior stateroom on this cruise, and while the space was a bit tight (I had a less maneuverable scooter at the time), we just had our steward remove some unnecessary furniture.

The public areas were very spacious, and there were many other passengers in wheelchairs, scooters, or walkers. This wasn't a surprise, as Celebrity tends to cater to an older demographic interested in comfort. Everything was just so easy to access and participate in, from theater performances to trivia to game shows to karaoke. I also loved the automatic doors at all public restrooms. I didn't use the pool, but was thrilled to see a permanently installed lift.

The Stats: Thirty accessible staterooms, no-threshold bathrooms and balconies, roll-in showers with fold-down benches, grab bars, lowered roll-under sinks, open bed frames, lifts at main pool and whirlpool, lowered casino tables, lowered bar counter, accessible route to tendering platform, reserved wheelchair seating in theaters.

Holland America Pinnacle Class

In February 2019, I sailed on Holland America's *MS Rotterdam*, which is the second oldest ship in the line's fleet. I'll admit, I had low expectations for a ship that was launched in 1997. It was heavily refurbished in 2017 to include many of the features in newer HAL ships, like America's Test Kitchen. The accessibility was surprisingly fantastic, so I couldn't wait to learn about the accessibility on HAL's newest ships.

The Pinnacle class includes the *MS Koningsdam* (2016) and the *MS Nieuw Statendam* (2018); the *MS Ryndam* will be joining them in May 2021. They're HAL's newest and largest ships, but still have a passenger capacity of less than 2,700 people. HAL's demographic leans heavily towards seniors, so the ambiance on HAL ships is luxurious, but mellow. Activities end by midnight and food service tends to end early as well. However, the accessibility on HAL ships is fantastic, as you'll have many fellow wheelchair, scooter, and walker users on board. Another fantastic thing about Holland America is that most of its ships have an accessible tendering system, allowing wheelchair users to disembark at tender ports (given good conditions).

The Stats: Twenty-seven fully accessible staterooms, thirteen ambulatory accessible rooms (shower only with small step. These rooms are designed for use by guests with mobility disabilities who do not require the regular use of a wheelchair, scooter, or other similar assistive devices), no-threshold bathrooms and balconies, roll-in showers with fold-down benches, grab bars, lowered roll-under sinks, open bed frames, lowered closet bars, lift at main pool (upon request with advance notice), reserved wheelchair seating in main theater.

6 SELECTING AN ITINERARY

Choosing an accessible cruise itinerary is probably the most daunting aspect of planning a vacation at sea. Many times, I have clients who contact me saying they want to go on a cruise somewhere sunny and warm, and that's all I have to work with. Even within the same cruise line and the same region, I may have the option of four different ships and maybe twenty different itineraries with only minor differences. So where do we even begin?

After having planned sixteen cruises for myself as a wheelchair user, and dozens more for clients in wheelchairs and their families, I've come up with the three most important factors to look at when choosing an accessible cruise itinerary.

First, it's important to select an itinerary where the majority of the ports of call are docked. There's no point in spending thousands of dollars on a cruise vacation when you can't even get off the ship at several stops. Taking a close look at the itinerary or contacting the cruise line directly will give you an idea of which ports are docked and which ports are tender-only. Even if your particular cruise ship has the capability of tendering wheelchair users, remember that the decision to allow this is ultimately up to the captain, who makes this determination based on the weather and the changing tides.

Second, you'll want an itinerary where there are accessible things to see and do. Some travelers are totally okay with just rolling off the ship and grabbing some food, drinks, and souvenirs in the shopping and dining village in the port. However, the point of a cruise for many passengers is to get out and explore a new city in a new country. It's good to find out if there are accessible attractions at most of the ports of call on an itinerary.

Third, knowing there are accessible attractions at a port of call is meaningless if you don't have a way to get to them. You'll need to find out if there are accessible shore excursions available at ports of call on an itinerary, either through the cruise line or through a third-party tour operator. It's also good to find out if you can just roll off the ship and into the city center nearby to explore independently, or the availability of accessible public transportation close to the port.

As an aside, you may also want to take into consideration where the itinerary starts and ends. I always recommend to my clients that they arrive at the embarkation city at least a day before the ship departs, especially if they have to fly overseas. Airlines are notorious for delays, and the last thing you want to do is miss your cruise because you cut it too close with your flight arrangements. You may want to look into the accessibility of the departure city to see if accessible hotels and transfers between the airport and the cruise port are available.

If all of this sounds like it involves a considerable amount of time to research, you are absolutely right. This is why I highly recommend working with an accessible travel agent to help you find the right itinerary. Many of us have personally been on several of these itineraries and have visited dozens of ports of call around the world. We also have partnerships with tour operators at different ports, and can give you an idea of what's available.

To give you an idea of what an itinerary like this would look like, here's my list of the best cruises for wheelchair users that include all three of the above features.

Royal Caribbean 8-Night Scandinavia and Russia. I went on this itinerary with Cory Lee of *Curb Free with Cory Lee* in August 2017, and it was fantastic! The *Jewel of the Seas* departs from Copenhagen (Denmark) and docks in Stockholm (Sweden), Tallinn (Estonia), St. Petersburg (Russia), and Helsinki (Finland). The ship is very wheelchair friendly, with large accessible staterooms, no-threshold balconies, pushbutton access to public toilets, and designated wheelchair spaces in the theater. Wheelchair accessible tours are available at each port of call, and while independent travel will be difficult to impossible in St. Petersburg (for both visa and logistical reasons), visitors can use accessible taxis, the Hop On-Hop Off bus, or public transportation at the other stops.

Princess 7-Day Alaska Inside Passage. I went on a slightly different version of this cruise in May 2016, and it was honestly one of the best travel experiences of my life. This itinerary is available on four Princess ships – the *Island, Star, Coral,* and *Golden* – depending on the departure date. It's a round-trip itinerary out of very wheelchair accessible Vancouver (which is worth an extra day's stay pre- and post-cruise) and stops in Juneau, Skagway, Glacier Bay (cruising), and Ketchikan.

Technically, Princess will tell you that you can dock or anchor at Juneau and Ketchikan. However, in my capacity as a travel agent, I learned directly from the Cruise Lines Agency of Alaska that Princess has priority over other cruise lines when it comes to docking. So, while a rare emergency may occur that requires Coast Guard vessels to take up precious docking space, chances are you'll be able to roll off the ship at every port with Princess.

Celebrity 12-Night Israel and Mediterranean. It's true that Celebrity is geared more towards bigger spenders. However, there's no doubt that the upper-tier cruise line keeps wheelchair users in mind when designing their ships. I went on a slightly different version of this cruise in November 2017, and everywhere I went on the ship (the *Silhouette* at the time), it felt like it was made just for me. The public spaces had more than ample room and designated spaces for wheelchair and scooter users – which is good, because there were a lot of us on that cruise.

The ship for this itinerary is the *Infinity*, which departs out of Rome (Italy) and ends in Athens (Greece). All ports of call are docked and include Naples (Italy), Catania (Sicily), Valetta (Malta), Rhodes (Greece), Ashdod/Jerusalem (Israel), Haifa (Israel), and Souda/Chania (Crete). Various tour operators offer wheelchair accessible shore excursions at every stop.

Royal Caribbean 7-Night Western Mediterranean. There are dozens of cruise itineraries that cover the western Caribbean, and most of them include the "biggies" in Spain, France, and Italy. However, most of them include at least one stop that requires tendering, so this particular cruise is a gem. It's also on the *Oasis of the Seas*, which is one of Royal's larger ships with a passenger capacity of over six thousand people. It has a lift for two of its pools and plenty of designated wheelchair seating throughout the ship.

The Oasis departs for its round-trip itinerary from the very wheelchair accessible city of Barcelona, and its all-docked ports of call include Palma de Mallorca (Spain), Marseilles/Provence (France), La Spezia/Florence/Pisa (Italy), Rome (Italy), and Naples (Italy). I highly recommend taking a few extra days to explore Barcelona with this itinerary.

Carnival 7-Night Southern Caribbean (from San Juan). Many travelers are hesitant to make cruise plans either out of or through Puerto Rico for fear of damage from Hurricane Maria. I can assure you that San Juan, as well as the vast majority of the Caribbean, is definitely open for business. This is a more economical itinerary on the Carnival *Fascination*, which is an older and mid-sized Fantasy-class ship, but it was given a huge overhaul in 2008 that made it shinier and more accessible, although its pools are unfortunately still lacking lifts. It also got a makeover in mid-February 2018 that added more dining options.

Ports of call include St. Thomas (US Virgin Islands), Barbados, St. Lucia, St. Kitts, and St. Maarten, all of which have accessible tours available through outside vendors. Carnival is a family and budget-oriented cruise line, so this itinerary would be ideal for couples with children not looking to break the bank.

Norwegian 5-Day Pacific Coastal. This one-way cruise from Vancouver to Los Angeles is a nice option for US-based travelers who want to stay close to home, and those who don't have the time to be away for a week or longer. This cruise also takes place on the *Norwegian Joy*, the line's newest ship, with this itinerary occurring in early October. All Norwegian ships have pool lifts, and younger family members in particular will enjoy the multiple water slides and two-deck go-cart race track.

Ports of call include Victoria, BC (Canada) and San Francisco, which means more great news for wheelchair users. Although Canada is not subject to US accessibility laws, it has its own wheelchair friendly laws that make Vancouver and Victoria nice options. San Francisco and Los Angeles are large cities, but they are subject to the ADA and have several choices for accessible tours and transportation.

Royal Caribbean Western Caribbean (from Miami). I love this itinerary for a couple of reasons. First, it's on the *Symphony of the Seas*, a cruise ship so new that the paint is probably still drying. That means it's super wheelchair accessible (including *three* pool lifts), and HUGE. It just happens to be the world's largest cruise ship at the moment, so chances are you're not going to run out of food to eat or things to do.

In addition to offering all-docked port stops at Costa Maya (Mexico), Cozumel (Mexico), and Coco Cay (Bahamas), it also stops in Roatán (Honduras), which isn't a typical port of call for a Western Caribbean itinerary. During accessible shore excursions, you can experience things like rides on beach wheelchairs, animal interactions, and scenic drives. This cruise is also family friendly, and ideal for large groups.

Princess 10-Day Eastern Caribbean Voyager (from Fort Lauderdale). I went on this cruise in November 2018 as my graduation reward from the Princess Academy. I went alone in my Whill Model Ci mobility device, which I thought would be a great test of the ship's accessibility, as well as that of the ports and tours. I really loved this itinerary because the ship docks at all six ports of call, and we also had three full days at sea to enjoy activities on the ship.

The *Crown Princess* is a bit older, but was recently refurbished and is absolutely lovely to see. The food is excellent, and I had no trouble rolling around the entire ship. I had a very spacious ocean view accessible stateroom that was definitely adequate for my needs. It took a bit of research, but I was able to find an accessible shore excursion at every port of call, which included Antigua, Martinique, St. Kitts, St. Thomas, Barbados, and Grand Turk.

7 ACCESSIBLE CRUISING IN THE CARIBBEAN

One of the most popular destinations for cruising is the Caribbean, and with good reason. It's a great place for families and summer vacations on the beach, the views are stunning, and it's a relatively inexpensive place to visit by cruise ship. I often recommend short 3-night cruises to the Bahamas to my clients who have never cruised before as a way to get their feet wet, so to speak. While many people still have to fly to Florida to go on a Caribbean cruise, for wheelchair users on the US East Coast who can't fly, at least it provides four major cruise ports within driving distance for many.

Virtually all the major cruise lines, and several of the smaller ones, offer Caribbean cruise itineraries. Typical ports of call, especially for the mega ships, include the Bahamas, Jamaica, Puerto Rico, the Virgin Islands, and Mexico. Wheelchair accessibility in the Caribbean is very limited, and more so on smaller islands. However, many cruise lines that sail in the Caribbean offer wheelchair accessible shore excursions. These are not private tours, but the groups tend to be smaller, which will save you some money compared to booking through a third-party tour operator. If you want more flexibility with your tour and are okay with spending more money, you can always book an accessible tour independently.

Keep in mind that some cruise lines will cancel an accessible shore excursion if not enough passengers sign up for them. Read the fine print to find out if this is a possibility for your cruise line. I've had this happen to me twice on the same cruise (MSC *Seaside*), and I had no alternate options for accessible transportation on such short notice. I've had much better luck with accessible shore excursions booked through Princess and Royal Caribbean.

Most of the major cruise lines have a private island in the Bahamas, which is included in many Caribbean itineraries. The only two private islands that currently have piers are Disney's Castaway Cay and Royal Caribbean's CocoCay. The former has good accessibility, but while they have dozens of beach wheelchairs, there are no beach mats where regular wheelchairs can roll on the sand.

The latter has made considerable improvements after wheelchair users complained about the lack of accessibility on CocoCay. However, much work needs to be done, as over half the island is not accessible to wheelchair users without transferring with assistance to a beach wheelchair. The good news is that many other ports of call for major cruise lines in the Caribbean are also docked. For a list of tender-only or part-time tender ports in the Caribbean, take a look at Appendix A.

What travelers love the most about the Caribbean is that temperatures are warm year-round. You won't see the typical four seasons, but rather two — wet season and dry season. While it is a good idea to carry a poncho or umbrella regardless of the time of year, even more important is wearing sunblock and carrying a way to keep cool if you are sensitive to high temperatures. Look for shade whenever possible, and carry a misting device or fan if possible.

With extremely few exceptions (like Martinique, where you need euros), all Caribbean island ports of call accept US dollars. Just be aware that small local vendors will probably give you cash back in the local currency. You can use your credit card in larger souvenir shops, restaurants, and many bars, but it's wise to have some cash on you at all times. If you don't bring it from home, you can usually get cash in US dollars in the casino ATM on board.

Navigating through large crowds of people and small spaces is always tricky for wheelchair users. Busy season for Caribbean cruises includes the summer months when kids are out of school, holidays like spring break, Thanksgiving, and Christmas, and the coldest winter months. Some cruise ports can have as many as five or six large cruise ships in port on a given day, which means that over twenty thousand cruise ship passengers can overwhelm a small port in a matter of hours. If you go on a group tour, be prepared to run into several other group tours from other ships at the same places. If you can afford a private tour, your guide will likely know how to time it so you can arrive either before or after larger groups.

These days, most Caribbean ports have a modern terminal area with several souvenir shops, restaurants, and bars. These are largely wheelchair accessible, as their goal is to maximize income from tourists from all walks of life. However, once you attempt to leave the immediate port area, you will likely be confronted with poor or a complete lack of wheelchair access due to crumbling sidewalks and/or a lack of dropped curbs depending on the location. Whenever possible, try to book an accessible shore excursion, either through the cruise line or independently. This may be difficult or impossible at some Caribbean ports of call, so determine how flexible you are in this regard when picking an itinerary.

Many tours in Caribbean ports of call include rum punch or other rum-infused drinks. Mixed beverages on the tours tend to be very strong, and usually not measured in a more conservative way like they are in the United States. Fortunately, while there have been many reported incidents of alcoholic beverages being spiked with the drugs at Mexican resorts, I haven't seen any such reports at Caribbean ports of call on tours. However, I have seen many tourists negatively affected by the combination of strong drinks on shore and the excessive heat and humidity. If you do drink while in port, make sure you stay hydrated with water as well.

Tour guides in the Caribbean work really hard every day to make sure that their guests are entertained and enjoying the sights. They don't make a lot of money, and you will see soon enough once you leave the port area the poor conditions that they probably live in. Unless your experience is really terrible, please have some extra cash on you and provide your guide with at least a small tip to show your gratitude.

Be wary of booking a Caribbean cruise during hurricane season, which runs from June 1 through November 30. Yes, it runs right through the summer high season. If a hurricane gets in the path of a cruise ship, the captain has several options for diverting to a different port. Please note you will not be refunded for your cruise if you skip a port due to a natural disaster or hurricane. I would, however, highly recommend purchasing a travel insurance policy if you plan to cruise during this time in case other parts of your vacation are affected. You can read more about travel insurance in Chapter 14.

Accessible Tour Operator Recommendations for the Caribbean

ICBW (St. Thomas)
Island Trams (Grand Turk)
This is Cozumel (Cozumel)
Bodden Tours (Roatan)
Kantours (St. Kitts)
Happy Taxi (Antigua)
Martinique Access'ile (Martinique)

8 ACCESSIBLE CRUISING IN THE MEDITERRANEAN

The Mediterranean Sea is probably my favorite place to cruise in the whole world. This region offers such a huge variety of experiences for wheelchair users, from accessible beaches near Barcelona to elevators in Rome's Colosseum. There are dozens of amazing cruise ports of call, and even more itineraries to consider. If you love history, beautiful architecture, museums, turquoise waters, and incredible scenery, then a Mediterranean cruise might be perfect for you.

Mediterranean cruise itineraries are commonly divided into Western and Eastern. They are further categorized into smaller geographic areas like the Greek Isles, Dalmatian Coast (Croatia), and Holy Land (Israel and Turkey). The Mediterranean Sea is a large body of water with many regions to explore by cruise, so it can be challenging to choose an itinerary.

Many people who embark on a Mediterranean cruise must get to the departure port by plane. Before taking a look at itinerary details, you may want to decide where you feel the most comfortable flying into and leaving for your cruise, especially since you'll likely want to spend at least one night there before your cruise. The wheelchair accessibility of departure ports for Mediterranean cruises can vary. I have sailed out of Rome (Civitavecchia) multiple times, as well as Venice. Barcelona and Athens (Piraeus) are two other common departure cities for Mediterranean cruises.

Having been to three of those cities as a wheelchair cruiser, and having arranged over a dozen cruises for clients out of the fourth, I can say unequivocally that Barcelona is the most accessible departure port city on the Mediterranean coast. Venice was such a joy to visit, and there are accessible hotel and transportation options in Rome and Athens. However, Barcelona is the least challenging (and probably the least expensive) for the combination of airport/cruise port transfers and hotel accommodations.

When it comes time to choose an itinerary, the hardest part may be deciding what you want to see and do. There are plenty of ports of call in the Mediterranean that are wheelchair accessible enough for you to enjoy major attractions. Do you want to visit larger European capitals? Get lost in the alleyways of an old medieval city? Take an excursion outside of the city into the countryside? Focus on the food and wine in a local area? Many people have had places like Rome or Athens on their bucket lists for a while, but others may not be familiar with the beauty of Croatia or Malta.

If you've managed to figure out what your priorities are for a Mediterranean cruise, then start taking a look at the accessibility of the ports of call. The majority of Mediterranean ports are docked, which is good news. For a list of tender ports in this region, take a look at Appendix A to help you weed those out if necessary. Then take a look at the geography of the port using Google Maps. Many city centers in the Mediterranean are easy to reach from the cruise ship dock without having to use transportation. If this is not the case, work with your cruise line or accessible travel agent to determine if any accessible shore excursions are available in that port.

Speaking of cruise lines, you may want to know which one is best for exploring the Mediterranean. Almost all major cruise lines have itineraries in this region, so I highly recommend that you take a look at Chapter 3 to see which cruise line fits your travel style the best. I will say that Celebrity and especially Holland America offer longer-duration itineraries, if that's what you're looking for. Luxury brands also tend to offer more immersive and educational opportunities onboard related to your different ports of call.

And speaking of shore excursions, in contrast with accessible tours in the Caribbean, Mediterranean shore excursions can be prohibitively expensive. Part of this is a supply and demand issue. In certain cities, there are only a handful of accessible vans or shuttles available to provide accessible tours. Another part of this is that in certain places, especially Italy, you are charged a premium for having a licensed tour guide, in contrast to a "travel assistant" who basically just keeps you company. If you want a licensed tour guide, you sometimes have to pay double what you would without one. You will pay this premium whether you book through the cruise line or book independently.

To get around this, take a look at itineraries where you can use a hop-on hop-off (HOHO) tour bus from close to the port, or public transportation to get you to the city center if rolling there is not an option. There are tons of audio and written walking/rolling tours that you can download for free from the Internet for cities all over the world. Not only will this save you money, but it will provide you with more freedom to wander. Another option, if you can transfer into and use a regular cab, is to hire a taxi driver on the spot to be your guide. They often offer similar tours as larger companies and cost a lot less.

Europe is pretty old, and while the countries you visit may have distinctly different histories and cultures, all of Europe has one thing in common—cobblestones. They are practically impossible to avoid anywhere you go in the Mediterranean, so just be prepared to encounter them at some point during your cruise. Most ports of call are welcoming to as many visitors as possible, so if you stick to the city center or tourist areas, you should find a decent number of curb cuts at intersections. Unfortunately, you may not be able to enter many souvenir shops or restaurants because of steps. However, outdoor seating is extremely common, and shopkeepers are more than happy to bring something outside for you to see.

Accessible Tour Operator and Travel Agent Recommendations for the Mediterranean

Disabled Accessible Travel (All Mediterranean)
Christianakis Travel (Greece)
Israel4All (Israel)
Turkey Accessible Travel (Turkey)

9 ACCESSIBLE CRUISING IN NORTHERN EUROPE

There are few sights in this world more stunning than the fjords of Norway. Equally impressive, but in a different way, are the palaces of St. Petersburg, the castles of Scotland, and the medieval towns of Estonia. These are all places that wheelchair users can visit on a variety of cruise itineraries in northern Europe. While my personal experience in this region is limited to the Baltic area, I will do my best to present you with information about cruise lines, itineraries, and ports of call.

Cruises in northern Europe have very different personalities than those in the Mediterranean. You will find itineraries that offer a lot more natural scenery, although there is plenty of history and old architecture to explore. With the exception of Disney, most major cruise lines offer itineraries in northern Europe. Common departure ports include Copenhagen, Stockholm, Amsterdam, and Southampton, with typical itineraries including the British Isles, the Baltic capitals, and Norwegian fjords. Some more adventurous itineraries head out to Iceland and even Greenland, but many of the ports of call there are tender-only.

As is the case with a Mediterranean cruise, ask yourself first what your priorities are for a Northern Europe cruise. If scenery is at the top of your list, then Norway's fjords are the way to go. If you're interested in detailed guided tours in larger cities with a focus on history, then the Baltic capitals might be right for you. If you're easing into international travel and aren't ready for a huge language or culture change, then a British Isles cruise may work better.

With regard to the accessibility of primary departure ports in northern Europe, I have only cruised out of Copenhagen. However, I have visited Stockholm, Amsterdam, and London, which is about forty-five minutes away from Southampton. Accessible taxis are in very limited supply in Copenhagen and Stockholm, although public transportation is good, and there are plenty of hotels with accessible rooms. Amsterdam is easier to manage, especially with the assistance of a local accessible tour operator. Although Southampton is a good distance away from London, it is a top option for a northern Europe departure port for wheelchair users.

Baltic cruise itineraries are a great choice for wheelchair users because ports of call, for the most part, are all docked. There are also accessible shore excursion options at most ports as well. Take note that they may be expensive in some cases, but you do have the HOHO bus option in Stockholm and Copenhagen. Please note that to disembark in Russia, you absolutely must have an organized tour arranged; rolling around on your own is not an option. Most likely that will be through an independent tour company, which will arrange your visas for you. This is a big deal, so make sure you communicate clearly with your local tour operator. You can also expect to wait at least one hour in line to go through Russian immigration, so factor that into your tour start time.

It's definitely possible to find a Norwegian fjords itinerary with all docked or mostly docked ports of call. In many cases, the city center is close enough to the port where you can roll into town without needing transportation. This is a plus because accessible taxis are not available in most of these ports, which are generally small towns, although public buses may be an option. Cobblestones can be brutal in some places, like Bergen, and you may have difficulty entering into shops or restaurants. If you're thinking about booking a Northern Lights cruise in the winter, please make sure that your mobility equipment is ready to deal with snow, ice, and very cold temperatures.

You will find more issues with tender-only ports on a British Isles cruise, as well as any itinerary that visits Iceland and Greenland. It's best to work with a local tour operator or your cruise line to determine where you can disembark, and how much there is for you to see and do. Accessibility in the United Kingdom overall is quite good, and you may be surprised at how many ancient sights and castles you'll be able to visit. I highly recommend any cruise itinerary that stops in Dublin or Belfast, as they are two my favorite northern European cities.

Accessible Tour Operator and Travel Agent Recommendations for Northern Europe

Disabled Accessible Travel (United Kingdom)
Accessible Travel Netherlands (Netherlands/Belgium)
Buitengewoon Reizen (Netherlands)
Undiscovered Britain (United Kingdom)
Iceland Unlimited (Iceland)
Saku Travel (Estonia)
I Love Travel SPB (St. Petersburg)
Happy Guide Helsinki (Helsinki)
Our Way Tours (Stockholm)

10 ACCESSIBLE CRUISING IN LATIN AMERICA

Home to the Panama Canal, the Amazon rainforest, Chilean fjords, and the gateway to Antarctica, it's no surprise that Latin America has some of the most sought-after cruise itineraries. Unfortunately, they are also some of the most challenging itineraries for wheelchair users. Some Latin America cruises are possible for people with mobility limitations, but please be aware that some compromises will need to be made. I have personally done a partial transit of the Panama Canal, but have not cruised around South America. As such, I will provide you with as much information as I can about itineraries, ports of call, and what you can expect based on my professional knowledge.

One of the most popular cruise itineraries in Latin America is the Panama Canal transit, either a full 14-day transit from east to west or vice versa, or a partial-transit round-trip itinerary, which usually runs about 10 days. the most common departure and arrival ports for canal cruises are Miami, San Diego, and Los Angeles. Many major cruise lines do canal itineraries, but only their smaller (and often older) ships are able to fit through all the locks for a full transit.

Panama Canal cruises stop in some pretty cool ports of call, like Cartagena (Colombia) and Limón (Costa Rica). I wasn't able to take a fully accessible tour in Cartagena, but I was able to store my disassembled power wheelchair in the trunk of a large sedan, and I also brought my portable travel ramp with me. Not every cruise passenger in a wheelchair can do this. I was, however, able to sign up for an accessible shore excursion through Princess in Costa Rica to the Veragua Rainforest Park, which used a coach bus with a lift.

Most ports of call on canal cruises will be docked, but most won't have accessible transportation options, either. In some cases, you may be able to roll to a nearby tourist market to buy some souvenirs or grab a bite to eat, but that's about it. That being said, the experience of watching almost the entire process of the Panama Canal transit was entirely worth my limited access to the ports of call on my cruise. Please make sure you review Appendix A to see which ports of call in Central America are tender only.

Cruise itineraries in and around South America tended to be longer — anywhere from 10 days to three or four weeks. With the exception of Disney, most major cruise lines sail in South America. However, you will tend to find the ships on these itineraries are smaller and perhaps a bit older. This is to make docking easier at popular ports of call in South America. Unfortunately, you will find that South America cruise itineraries have a considerable amount of tender-only ports, particularly near the southern tip of the continent.

The most common South America cruise itinerary is a one-way journey, starting in Valparaiso, Chile and ending in Buenos Aires, Argentina (or the reverse). One of my professional colleagues, a triple amputee in a larger power wheelchair, has spent some time in Buenos Aires, so I know that accessibility is good enough for a wheelchair user to spend some time there, and likely embark on a cruise with the assistance of a local accessible tour operator. Santiago is the closest major city to Valparaiso on the coast, about an hour's drive west. I'm entirely unfamiliar with the accessibility in Santiago. However, at the bottom of this chapter, you will find links to two different accessible tour operators that may be able to assist you with accommodations and transfers in Santiago.

Typical ports of call include Montevideo, the Falkland Islands, Ushuaia, Punta Arenas, and Puerto Montt. Midsize cruise ships from the major lines have to tender at most of these ports. Please review Appendix A to see all the tender-only ports in South America. There are smaller ships from smaller cruise lines, like Azamara or Seabourn, that can dock in some of these places. However, wheelchair accessibility onboard smaller ships is significantly reduced, and accessible shore excursions and transportation are typically not available ashore.

One of the biggest bucket list items for more adventurous wheelchair travelers is visiting the seventh continent, Antarctica. On a major cruise line on a typical midsize ship, setting foot or wheel on the Antarctic continent as a wheelchair user is currently impossible. The ship must anchor, and excursions usually utilize Zodiac rafts. I've heard of more able-bodied manual wheelchair users being carried in their chair onto a Zodiac raft, then carried on to land. However, this was on a very small expedition vessel. I don't see a situation where the captain of a regular cruise ship would allow this. If your goal, however, is just to lay eyes on Antarctica, then that's totally possible, as the cruise ships sail close enough to land.

Accessible Tour Operator and Travel Agent Recommendations for Latin America

Latinamerica For All (Ecuador/Peru/Argentina)
Korke (Chile/Argentina)

11 ACCESSIBLE CRUISING IN ASIA-PACIFIC

This is easily the toughest part of the world for Americans to reach in order to embark on a cruise. However, cruising in Asia or around the Pacific Ocean can be an incredible experience worth dozens of hours spent on planes and in airports. While Asia in general is difficult with regard to wheelchair accessibility, there are some pretty cool opportunities to explore specific areas by cruise ship. I have visited many parts of the Asia-Pacific region on land, but not as part of a cruise. As such, I will provide you with as much information as I can about itineraries, ports of call, and what you can expect based on my professional knowledge.

There are dozens of cruise itineraries available across Asia and the Pacific. Most major cruise lines offer itineraries in this region, although some specialize in certain countries more than others. You can also find itineraries as brief as four nights, or as long as several weeks. In this chapter, I'm going to focus on the four sub-regions that have the most potential for wheelchair accessibility: Hawaii, Japan/Korea, Australia/New Zealand, and Southeast Asia.

Before narrowing down to a sub-region for your cruise, you may want to decide which departure port will be easiest for you to reach and manage. The most common departure ports for Asia-Pacific cruises are Honolulu, Singapore, Tokyo (Yokohama), Hong Kong, Sydney, and Auckland. With the exception of Tokyo, I've been to all of these cities, and the wheelchair accessibility ranges from very good to outstanding. Accessibility aside, your deciding factor may come down to budget and flight convenience.

Hawaii is definitely the easiest destination in the Pacific Ocean for wheelchair users, largely because it's a US state subject to the Americans with Disabilities Act. There are a few major cruise lines that cruise to Hawaii on longer 10-night to 17-night itineraries from the US West Coast, usually including either a departure from Seattle or San Diego with a stop in Victoria (Canada) or Ensenada (Mexico).

In order to comply with the Jones Act, all foreign-flagged vessels departing from the United States must stop in at least one foreign port before returning to a US port. It's generally too expensive to flag a cruise ship in the United States to avoid this, but Norwegian Cruise Lines has one exception — the *Pride of America*. This is the only vessel that can do round-trip tours in Hawaii that both depart from and arrive in Hawaiian ports. If you don't want to deal with several days at sea making the crossing from California to Hawaii, it's possible to fly to Honolulu and take a seven-night cruise on the *Pride of America.*

I'm not familiar with any tour operators or specific accessible tours in Hawaii. That being said, public buses in Hawaii are wheelchair accessible, so taking public transportation (especially in Honolulu) is an inexpensive option. Because of ADA laws, it should be easy to explore parts of Hawaiian ports on your own, and hopefully easy to find a shore excursion that includes a coach bus or shuttle with a lift.

Many cruise itineraries in Australia and New Zealand combine stops in both countries, sometimes including the island of Tasmania. Some travelers who don't know much about Australia significantly underestimate its size. Australia is roughly the same size as the United States, so it can take two weeks or longer to circle the country on a cruise ship. There are shorter itineraries available between Sydney and New Zealand, but the number of port stops in Australia will be more limited.

I am not familiar with the specifics of available accessible shore excursions in either Australia or New Zealand. However, having visited both countries, I can tell you that wheelchair accessibility is generally quite good, particularly in larger cities. There are also accessible tour providers in both countries that you can contact (links below) to see if they can offer accessible shore excursions for your cruise. Please keep in mind that at some ports of call in both countries, the city center may be some distance away from the port, and you will have to research the availability of accessible taxis or public transportation.

Cruise itineraries in Japan offer a considerable amount of flexibility, with cruises as brief as two nights to as long as several weeks. Many Japan itineraries also include stops in South Korea. Some ports of call in Japan are tender-only, so please review Appendix A to take these into account. While wheelchair accessibility is good, from what I understand, in Japan's larger cities, this is not always the case in smaller ports. I would suggest reaching out to one of the accessible tour operators below to see what your options are for accessible shore excursions in Japan.

I have had very good experiences with wheelchair accessibility in Seoul, South Korea. Several major cruise lines dock in Incheon, and it's about an hour's drive to reach Seoul from the port. Reach out to the tour provider below to determine your options for any wheelchair accessible shore excursions to Seoul from Incheon. Another major port of call in South Korea is Busan, the country's second-largest city. I'm not familiar with accessibility there, but I understand that they have a HOHO bus that may be accessible, as well as a metro and public bus service.

The most challenging ports of call for wheelchair users will be in Southeast Asia, specifically countries like Vietnam, Thailand, and Cambodia. There are more accessible tour operators now available in this area that offer shore excursions. However, there are many tender-only ports, especially in Thailand. Please review Appendix A to take these into account when selecting an itinerary. Also, please reach out to one of the tour operators listed below to determine your options for accessible shore excursions in Southeast Asia.

Accessible Tour Operator and Travel Agent Recommendations for Asia Pacific

Accessible New Zealand (New Zealand)
Korea Wheelchair Tour (Seoul)
Wheelchairs to Go (Sydney)
Accessible Japan (Japan)
Accessible Indonesia (Indonesia)
Roll in Asia (Vietnam/Myanmar/Cambodia/Japan)

12 ACCESSIBLE CRUISING IN ALASKA

An Alaska cruise is one of the most common bucket list items for travelers, especially those in their retirement years. It is arguably also the easiest way to visit The Last Frontier in America. Having cruised to Alaska in 2016, this is still one of my favorite destinations in the entire world—and I've been to the Swiss Alps. Considering the volume of Alaska cruises I book for my clients, it's a popular itinerary for wheelchair users as well. This shouldn't come as a surprise, considering that as a US state, Alaska falls under the guidance of the Americans With Disabilities Act.

The scenery is jaw-dropping, and the people are so friendly and welcoming. There are also several offerings for accessible shore excursions at virtually every port of call. However, there are a few things to take into consideration when picking the right cruise ship itinerary for an Alaska cruise. You can sail round-trip, or one-way northbound or southbound. With most cruise lines, you can add on a multi-day land portion of a cruise tour, which typically includes a stay at a lodge, possibly a train ride to see Denali, or a coach bus tour to see wildlife.

One of the first things you want to decide is where you want to depart for your Alaska cruise. You will also need to decide if you want your cruise to be round-trip or one-way. The majority of Alaska cruises depart from either Seattle, Washington or Vancouver, British Columbia. These are typically seven-night itineraries. There are also a few one-way itineraries that depart from San Francisco and Long

Beach, California, and these are either 10-night, 12-night, or 14-night itineraries.

The one-way itineraries often arrive in either Seward or Whittier, both of which have connections to Anchorage and often side excursions by train to visit places like Denali National Park. It is often more expensive to fly into the departure port and fly out of the arrival port, so keep this in mind when budgeting. I usually recommend to my clients that they arrive at the departure port at least one day prior to the cruise sailing date. Both Vancouver and Seattle offer several great options for wheelchair accessible hotel rooms.

Many Alaska cruise itineraries are similar from cruise line to cruise line with only minor variations. They usually involve three or four ports of call and cruising through one of the many glacier viewing areas where the sea is like glass. Typical ports of call include Juneau, Ketchikan, Skagway, Victoria, Icy Strait Point, and Sitka. What is crucial for wheelchair travelers to know and understand is that some ports of call in Alaska itineraries are tender only, and many others are either "dock or anchor" (D/A).

This means that most likely you will be stuck on the ship when you are at a tender port. In places like Juneau or Ketchikan, the ship can either dock or anchor, depending on many factors. Some cruise lines have much better chances of docking on certain days. Cruise Lines of Alaska (CLA) makes this determination each year, and publishes a schedule in roughly late November of which ships will be docking in Alaska ports and which will be anchoring; this is, of course, subject to change.

Most of the bigger cruise lines, like Norwegian, Holland America, and Princess, have fully accessible ships on Alaska itineraries. However, some are newer and better than others. Each cruise line has a special needs department you can contact for accessible stateroom details (see Appendix B). For example, I booked a balcony cabin on the Star Princess, and the threshold from the room to the balcony was too high for me to negotiate with my scooter. However, on a Royal Caribbean cruise in Scandinavia, the threshold was completely flat. These are the kinds of questions you want to ask before selecting a ship and a cabin.

Alaska itineraries tend to be more expensive compared to other cruises, so it's important that you have a realistic expectation of what an Alaska cruise will cost. One of the primary cost factors is the cruise line. Generally speaking, Carnival will be the least expensive and Disney will be the most expensive, with Royal Caribbean and Norwegian at the lower end and Princess, Holland America, Celebrity, and Cunard at the upper end.

Another major cost factor is the type of stateroom you prefer. Accessible staterooms cost exactly the same as a regular stateroom in an identical category and location on the ship. Your least expensive option will be an interior stateroom. Balconies are *extremely* popular on Alaska sailings because you can view the glaciers in the comfort and privacy of your own stateroom without having to fight the crowd for space on deck. However, balconies cost more and sell out first. When you sail will also affect your cost. Mid-summer is the high season and most expensive, while you can get cheaper fares in May and September. To accommodate for taxes, port fees, and gratuities, I would budget no less than $1,500 per person for an interior stateroom and $2,000 for a balcony stateroom.

Assuming you've chosen an itinerary with all docked ports of call, here are my picks for the top wheelchair accessible shore excursions or tours to take during your Alaska cruise.

Ketchikan

The Great Alaskan Lumberjack Show. You can find the entrance to this one-hour show right across from the cruise ship dock. The show takes place in a small open-air amphitheater, and there are several spaces in the front reserved for wheelchair users and their companions. It's comprised of two competing teams, one from Canada and one from the United States. They take part in all sorts of lumberjack events involving cutting tools and large pieces of wood, with no small amount of smack talking and comedic gestures. It's only a little over an hour long, but it was absolutely hilarious and very family-friendly. You can also take some fun pictures with the lumberjacks afterward! This tour can be booked through your cruise line.

The "Deadliest Catch" Crab Fishermen's Tour. Over the course of three hours, you'll learn how fishermen in the waters off the coast of Alaska catch various kinds of fish and Alaskan King crab. You will also learn why the Discovery Channel show is called "Deadliest Catch." The stories the tour guides told us were absolutely mesmerizing and terrifying all at once. However, the best part of the tour was when we stopped just off the coast of a small island controlled by a small local Native American tribe. There must have been hundreds of bald eagles waiting in the trees for us. The tour guides started cutting up pieces of fish, and tossing them into the water.

And that was when the show began! Imagine anywhere between fifty to one hundred wild bald eagles coming in and grasping these pieces of fish out of the water with their huge talons. It was absolutely awe-inspiring. I had no trouble being rolled to the edge of the boat to watch, or to get to and from a comfortable place for the entire tour. I don't know if I would have been able to go to the bathroom, but since the tour was only three hours I didn't have to worry about it, fortunately. The tour guides were so incredibly nice and made sure that all my needs were taken care of. This tour can be booked through your cruise line.

Juneau

Mount Roberts Tramway. The Goldbelt Mount Roberts Tramway opened in 1996 and operates May through September. It is the only aerial tramway in southeast Alaska, and is a short roll from the cruise ship dock. Cars rise 1,800 feet from the dock in downtown Juneau through the rain forest to the Mountain House, offering expansive views of Juneau and Gastineau Channel. The Mount Roberts Tramway is one of the most vertical tramways in the world and received the Governor's Award for facility accessibility design. It is fully ADA compliant and can easily accommodate guests with accessibility requirements. The Nature Center at the top invites you to even enjoy a cup of cider while you muse around many interpretive displays or browse through their gift shop for unique nature-oriented gifts, books, and maps. You can purchase your tramway tickets at the visitor center.

Mendenhall Glacier Explorer. Your journey begins with a narrated tour of downtown Juneau and the city's highlights en route to Mendenhall Valley — home of the mighty Mendenhall Glacier. Your guide will point out many of the attractions that you'll want to see during your approximate two-hour stay at the glacier area. Scenic Photo Point and the Mendenhall Glacier Visitor Center are well worth a visit. Take time to watch the short film about the glacier and the thirty-seven other glaciers that make up the Juneau Ice Field. The area boasts several self-guided scenic trails that allow you to learn about the role the glacier had in carving the landscape.

Each of these trails offers a different view of the Mendenhall through trees or along the shores of Mendenhall Lake. The Nugget Falls trail takes you to the base of a long glacier-fed waterfall and offers the closest views of Mendenhall Glacier in the area. Meander through the Tongass National Forest as you explore the Moraine Ecology Trail and the Steep Creek Trail — the latter offers multiple views of wild sockeye salmon during the mid- to late-summer months. This tour can be booked through your cruise line. Book well in advance and make sure you select the wheelchair accessible option so you will be provided with a bus with a lift.

Dolphin Jet Boat Tours. What is it about whales? Nothing makes you feel so powerfully alive as the sight of one, especially in an intimate setting and at close range — like what you'll find with Dolphin Jet Boat Tours. You can hear the air blasting through the blowholes as the massive creature rises from the water, mist floating through the air and dampening your face. And you won't get this feeling on a crowded, less personal tour boat. Their tours are operated under special use permit in the Tongass National Forest. The boats are enclosed and climate-controlled for comfort, with large outside decks, a restroom, and comfortable forward-facing seats. The boats have water-propelled jets, so they're fast. They are an equal opportunity service provider. Anyone needing special accommodation or accessibility should inquire at least seventy-two hours in advance to ensure they will be able to meet your needs. These tours must be booked independently.

Sitka

Birds, Bears, & Barnacles. The town of Sitka is located on a small but very scenic island off the coast of mainland Alaska. In the late 1800s it was controlled by Russia, so it has a large Russian cultural influence. We signed up for this accessible tour that took us to a birds of prey rehabilitation center, where we got to see bald eagles up close. It was absolutely amazing! There were also many other species of raptors at the center in different stages of recovery from various injuries.

After that, we went to a rehabilitation facility for bears. They had grizzly bears and black bears, and there were also many bald eagles just flying around like it was no big deal. Maybe for them, but for me it was absolutely incredible to see our national symbol just flying around in the wild. Our third and final stop was at a small aquarium and fish hatchery. After you book this shore excursion, you will have to call the company directly to let them know you will need an accessible shuttle bus with a lift for the tour.

Skagway

White Pass & Yukon Route Railway. The Skagway White Pass Railroad Summit Excursion is easily the most popular Skagway shore tour. You'll take an unforgettable journey aboard the "Scenic Railway of the World" to the White Pass summit. Begin your excursion as you board the train in Skagway and travel twenty miles from tidewater, to the Summit of the White Pass — a 2,865-foot elevation Every passenger enjoys vast canyon views and complimentary bottled water throughout the fully narrated tour. Relax in vintage passenger coaches as you retrace the original route to the White Pass summit, passing Bridal Veil Falls, Inspiration Point, and Dead Horse Gulch.

Enjoy a breathtaking panorama of mountains, glaciers, gorges, waterfalls, tunnels, trestles, and historic sites along the White Pass Railroad. See the original Klondike Trail of 1898 worn into the rocks, a permanent tribute to the thousands of souls who passed this way in search of fortune. All Summit Excursion trains are wheelchair accessible. However, space is limited in lift-equipped cars. After you book this shore excursion, you will have to call the company directly to let them know you will need a wheelchair accessible spot on the train.

Victoria

London Taxi Tours. This Victoria tour company has been provided guided tours to visitors to this beautiful Canadian city for over eight years and is now able to offer their outstanding services to people with mobility issues in their fully accessible van. Whether it is a tour to beautiful Butchart Gardens, a city tour, or a wine tour to other areas of our Island, now the whole family can travel in comfort. With your own personal driver and guide, you can see Victoria at your own pace. Stop for pictures wherever you want, decide how long to stay at each stop, take a pre-determined tour or plan your own itinerary. Whether it is a 4-Hour Grand City Tour, a half-day Wine Tour, or a Tour to Butchart Gardens, they can be of service. This tour must be booked independently.

13 ACCESSIBLE RIVER CRUISING

River cruises offer some of the most spectacular scenery in the world. Popular on several continents, the ships are small, intimate, and often quite luxurious. The bad news is that river cruises are almost completely off-limits for full-time and power wheelchair users. However, people with some mobility can make a river cruise work with some flexibility, assistance, and advance planning. The great news is that there are fully accessible charter cruise options for Holland and Germany for wheelchair users willing to forgo some luxury options in favor of the amazing opportunity to cruise Europe's stunning rivers. Read below to find out if river cruising is right for you and your mobility needs.

General Considerations

Most companies only allow wheelchairs that are collapsible. Some do not allow motorized wheelchairs. Solo travel is generally not an option, and you will likely be required to travel with another passenger who can assist you. When your boat docks at each new port, there may be times when you will not be able to leave the ship if you are unable to walk and must be carried on and off the boat in a wheelchair. If the cruise line staff is unable to assist and determines it's unsafe, you will be required to stay on the ship at that port. Some of the tours, particularly in Europe, require a lot of walking across cobblestone streets, up many stairs and hills, and through narrow passageways both inside and outside buildings. However, you may be able to book an accessible tour independently, depending on the port of call.

Even though some companies have designated cabins for accessible travel, there are a limited number available on each ship. Each cruise company also varies with the level of assistance they will provide with regard to airport transfers, getting on and off the ship, making special accommodations for tours and excursions, and other things not mentioned. Many river ship cabins can only accommodate two people, and the cruises cater to a much older crowd. As such, there are no kids' programs, and some river cruises are adults-only. However, more river cruise lines understand that cruising has become a multi-generational endeavor, and are providing more suites that either can accommodate more people or connect to each other.

Embarkation/Debarkation

River ships all share docking ports in Europe. Throughout your cruise, it is likely the ship will be docked next to one or two other river ships. During this time, your view from your stateroom may temporarily be obscured by a neighboring ship. It is important to note that in these cases, disembarkation and/or embarkation may include walking through the adjacent ship's lobby or upper deck to reach the shore. Most lines specify that wheelchair users have to be accompanied by someone who can assist them and be responsible for their embarkation and disembarkation. Despite this official line, crew members will often lend a hand — but this can never be guaranteed as river vessels have a relatively small number of staff, and nobody will be assigned to help disabled passengers.

Staterooms

Riverboat cabins are much smaller than hotel rooms, and not every river ship offers accessible staterooms. Several lines offer a small number of accessible or modified staterooms with wide doors, but these might not be available on each of their ships. You'll want to know if it's easy to open the door and go inside with a wheelchair, and if there is enough space to store a wheelchair and other mobility aids. (Equipment cannot be stored in the corridors due to safety regulations, and most lines stipulate that passengers have to bring collapsible wheelchairs.) Some shower stalls have fixed doors with limited access, while others have handy doors that fold right back to create one large area of bathroom space. You'll need to inquire about bathroom configuration — especially if you're not booking a special accessible room.

River Cruise Ship Layouts

River cruise ships are much smaller than ocean vessels, particularly in Europe, where they are restricted in width and length to fit into locks and sail beneath low bridges, and parts of Asia where they have to navigate shallow waters. Most have a maximum capacity of 250 passengers or less, and typically only have three or four decks. Many river cruise ships have several dining options, several bars and lounges, a swimming pool, and even a cinema and salon.

There is generally an open-seating policy for dining, so you can sit where you want. Meals can be fairly regimented due to the small size of the galley, so one sitting for breakfast, lunch, and dinner is the norm (although some lines are more flexible with timings than others). Lighter meals can be enjoyed in the lounge or outside on the deck, and some vessels have additional specialty restaurants. Entertainment is low-key, with the major attraction being the passing scenery.

Itineraries and Ports of Call

European river cruises travel along the Rhine, Danube, and Seine Rivers, as well as other major waterways. A great deal of effort is made to ensure guests enjoy food and wine of the specific region being traveled. International cruises vary in length from a week to three weeks, with a select few longer in duration. In many river cruise ports of call, museums, churches, shops, restaurants and other attractions are usually very close by, with no need for bus transfers. Viking, in particular, has prime central mooring spots, as it owns its own docks. However, this isn't the case in many European cities. Sometimes bridges are too low for river cruise ships to make it into the heart of town. Other factors that can influence where a ship docks include its size — the Viking Longships are too big to dock in central Paris, for example — and the agreement that the line has (or doesn't have) with the local harbor authorities.

Look for cruise lines that grade their guided walking tours according to fitness levels; slower walks that don't involve any steps are usually suitable for people in wheelchairs and with restricted mobility. The bad news is that many of Europe's old towns have cobbled streets, which can present problems. The cruise director will be able to advise which tours are suitable for different individuals, based on their mobility. He or she will also be able to suggest places where disabled passengers can rest, or see an alternative attraction with wheelchair access, or if parts of the trip (such as castle visits) involve long walks and uneven steps. For longer trips involving bus travel, coaches are not adapted for wheelchair use, so passengers need to be able to lift wheelchairs and mobility aids onto the bus and be able to climb the steps onto the vehicle.

For passengers who are full-time wheelchair users, or have very limited mobility, it is best to choose itineraries that cover longer distances with plenty of cruising time. This means they will be able to spend more time aboard with fellow passengers. Top options — and also an excellent choice for first-time cruisers — are sailings on the Rhine and Danube, the most popular rivers in Europe.

Water Level Considerations

Most cruises sail ahead with no interruptions on the river. However, Mother Nature occasionally presents river cruises with unexpectedly high or low water levels outside of the line's control. They are always prepared to make any necessary modifications during these unforeseen events to provide passengers with a memorable experience. Modifications may include temporary hotel accommodations and additional bus rides to cities through which the ship cannot sail.

Accessibility Information by Cruise Line

[This information was obtained from the cruise lines' websites, and was current at the time of this publication. Double-check the site again before you book your river cruise.]

AmaWaterways

AmaWaterways does allow mobility scooters onboard; the cruise line prefers foldable scooters, and they must be notified in advance of any arrangement made with a third-party supplier.

Europe: Wheelchair accessibility is very limited on their European ships. They do have an elevator between the two main decks, but it does not reach the Sun deck or Piano deck. Wheelchair users would be able to move around the dining room and lounge in their chairs. However, the cabins are not able to accommodate a wheelchair, so while in your stateroom, you would need to be able to move around on your own. Your chair would also need to be stored in your stateroom, due to limited storage on board.

Getting on and off the ship could be a challenge, as the planks are narrow and cannot accommodate a wheelchair or scooter's width. You would have to be able to get on and off the ship without your wheelchair, which would have to be light enough to be lifted off and on the ramps. It is common to tie up to other river ships in port. When this happens, passengers would sometimes need to travel through another ship to disembark, with many ships requiring they do so from the Sun deck, where there is only stair access. There are no medical facilities on board. However medical services can easily be called from shore if required.

Vietnam & Cambodia: These itineraries require a person to be able-bodied. There are many unpaved roads and the ships do not have elevators. They do not employ doctors or nurses on board the ships. In the event medical assistance is needed, appropriate medical facilities will be contacted. Note that response time can vary.

Africa: The *Zambezi Queen* cruising the Chobe River does not feature an elevator. They do not employ doctors or nurses on board the *Zambezi Queen*. In the event medical assistance is needed, appropriate medical facilities will be contacted. Note that response time can vary.

Viking River Cruises

Viking welcomes disabled guests, but points out challenges that exist onboard and during shore excursions. Viking does not have any designated wheelchair accessible cabins. Most ships have elevators; some ships have split-level decks and/or significant thresholds that could make movement difficult. Shore excursions often include walking over cobblestones, or up and down stairs.

Physically challenged guests require the services of a traveling companion who can help with all their needs since crew availability is limited in most circumstances. Collapsible wheelchairs are allowed, but motorized scooters cannot be accommodated. Viking Cruise Line does not allow mobility scooters on their international river cruise sailings. Viking allows collapsible wheelchairs and canes, which must be kept in the individual's stateroom.

Emerald Waterways

Emerald Sky and Emerald Star each have one wheelchair accessible cabin, located next to reception so passengers have easy access to and from their rooms. The elevators on Emerald ships service three out of four decks, with access to the sun deck only possible using stairs. Sightseeing in many historic towns and cities can only be undertaken by walking tours of up to 5 kilometers (3.2 miles), often on uneven surfaces.

Some tours include mountain excursions involving high altitudes. Consequently, a reasonably adequate (and sometimes high) level of fitness is required for many of their tours. Please consult with your doctor to ensure that you have an adequate level of fitness and are in good health before participating in these included excursions. Emerald will not provide any refunds if you are not able to participate in any portion of the tour. Most transportation services are not equipped with elevators or wheelchair ramps, and cabin doors and restrooms may not be wide enough to provide access for standard wheelchairs.

Emerald will make reasonable attempts to accommodate the special needs of its physically challenged guests, but is not responsible in the event it is unable to do so. Nor is it responsible for any denial of service by vessel operators, air carriers, hotels, restaurants or other providers. They cannot provide individual assistance to customers for walking, dining, getting on and off vessels, motorcoaches and other vehicles, or for other personal needs. A qualified and physically able companion must accompany travelers who need assistance and must assume full responsibility for their well-being. Please note that motorized scooters are not suitable on international tours, and are may not be permitted in certain countries.

Uniworld

Wheelchair-accessible staterooms are not available; however, all shower stalls are equipped with grab bars. Most ships have an elevator to serve passenger decks, and a chair lift leading to the sun deck. Travel-sized, collapsible wheelchairs can be used onboard, and there is a "gentle walking" shore excursion program offered in select locations. The line asks that all passengers should be able to walk unassisted in order to participate in guided tours and, if a wheelchair is necessary for use ashore, then guests are recommended to explore independently. Uniworld will review scooters and wheelchairs on a case-by-case basis and are as flexible as possible. Uniworld allows walkers, canes and oxygen concentrators.

Uniworld, at its sole discretion, reserves the right to refuse passage or to require a current passenger to end his or her trip if the passenger's state of health or physical condition may affect his or her own health, safety and enjoyment, or that of other passengers.

Scenic

Scenic provides "limited mobility suites" situated near the reception desk on all its ships. These feature a wide, wheelchair-accessible door; a bathtub with grab handles; and wheel-in shower with a stool and wall rail. Ships have elevators serving the passenger decks, but not the sun deck. Some excursions are wheelchair accessible. Scenic Cruising does allow mobility scooters, folding is preferred, kept inside a guest's cabin, but does not allow them to be used on board, only on land. For safety precautions, the passengers must be able to embark and disembark the vessel without the assistance of the scooter.

Avalon

Most stateroom and bathroom doors, as well as restrooms, are not wide enough to allow access by standard wheelchairs, and bathrooms and other doorways may be fitted with coamings. Motorized scooters and motorized wheelchairs are not permitted on Avalon cruises.

Arrangements cannot be made to carry or use these on tour or cruise, and if you bring one, you will be asked to make alternate arrangements for transporting the scooter to your end destination at your expense. Collapsible wheelchairs are permitted on board, but for safety reasons, the number Avalon can accept is limited.

Maximum wheelchair size must not exceed 1030mm/40.55" length x 555mm/21.85" width. You must notify Avalon at the time of booking of your intention to bring a wheelchair to ensure Avalon can accommodate it within safety regulations. Otherwise, you or your wheelchair may not be permitted on board. There is no separate storage for wheelchairs; it must be kept in your stateroom. For safety reasons, passengers in wheelchairs cannot be carried on ramps in ports where the ship is at anchor.

There are elevators on Scenery and Panorama-class ships, excluding access to the sun deck. Members of the crew will provide as much help as they can, but a single crew member cannot be assigned to someone with mobility issues for the duration of the cruise. Anyone with mobility issues is requested to fill out a detailed questionnaire prior to the cruise, so the line can ensure it can accommodate them and fulfill their individual needs. Some local walking tours from the ship are suited to wheelchair users who have an able-bodied companion.

You must report to Avalon any disability requiring special attention while on tour or on cruise at the time the reservation is made. Avalon will make reasonable efforts to accommodate the special needs of disabled passengers, but is not responsible in the event it is unable to do so nor responsible for any denial of services by air carriers, hotels, restaurants, or other independent suppliers. A qualified and physically able companion should accompany passengers who need such assistance.

If Avalon is not notified at time of reservation of any disability requiring special attention, Avalon reserves the right to cancel your booking or terminate your vacation if your special needs or disabilities are not suitable for the vacation, pose a threat to the health and safety of other participants or personnel on board the vessel, are incompatible with other passengers, or if you are not traveling with a companion who provides all the assistance you require. Avalon will not refund or cover any costs or expenses incurred for cancellation, booking, or termination of the vacation. Cancellation penalties, as above, apply.

CroisiEurope

All of CroisiEurope's premium-rated ships offer accessible cabins with wide doors and equipment for passengers with mobility issues. The three-deck ships have elevators that go to all floors except the sun deck. Disabled passengers need to travel with an adult who can assist them, as crew availability is limited. Passengers are encouraged to contact the line in advance, so it can recommend the most suitable vessel for their specific needs.

Any passenger with a physical or mental incapacity, limited capacity of mobility, having an illness requiring treatment or medical care, or pregnant women should inform the travel agent at the time of booking. No reservations can be accepted for passengers whose physical or mental condition is likely to render their participation in the cruise or in the vacation impossible or dangerous for themselves or others, or who require forms of care or assistance impossible to guarantee aboard ship, notably because of unsuitable infrastructure. Some suppliers (hoteliers, airlines and cruise companies, etc) may require a medical certificate confirming that the passenger is fit to travel or they may refuse to accept the booking if they feel that they will be unable to guarantee any assistance or treatment deemed necessary for the health and well-being of the passenger.

Participation in the voyage and in excursions is subject to the condition of the passenger having sufficient mobility. If necessary, the disabled may be accompanied at their own expense to obtain the required assistance. If CroisiEurope considers it strictly necessary for the safety and comfort of the passenger, bookings of persons with disabilities or reduced mobility will be subject to the condition that a companion able to assist the disabled or mobility-impaired passenger be present. This requirement is entirely dependent on CroisiEurope's assessment of the safety related needs of the disabled or mobility-impaired passenger and may vary from one route to another and/or from one boat to another.

If the disabled or reduced mobility person requests and requires special assistance (care, supervision), they must be accompanied by a companion who can provide the required assistance at their own expense. All personal accidents, diversions or forced stopover costs disrupting the course of the cruise shall be at the liability of the passenger having concealed his unfitness to travel.

Vantage

Ships are equipped with a hydraulic chair between the top passenger deck and sun deck, and there are elevators serving all the inside decks. *Discovery II* has an accessible cabin and all ships have an accessible restroom in the public area. Passengers also have access to extra wheelchairs that are carried onboard. The line's policy is that all disabled passengers must be accompanied by someone who can be fully responsible for helping them on and off the vessel and tour buses.

American Cruise Lines

American Cruise Lines itineraries include 7-, 8-, 10-, and 14-day cruises of the New England islands, Chesapeake Bay, historic antebellum South, Maine coast and harbors, Mid-Atlantic Inland Passage, Hudson River, Potomac & Delaware Rivers, rivers of Florida; seven-night Columbia and Snake River cruises of one thousand miles along the Lewis & Clark Route, Oregon Trail, and parts of the Pacific Northwest; and round-trip Alaska cruises from Juneau, and between Juneau and Seattle.

On the *American Spirit*, lounges, sundecks, and dining salons are accessible by wheelchairs or other walking aid devices. The ship is also equipped with an elevator for ease of movement between decks. One cabin is designated as wheelchair accessible. The *Queen of the West* has two wheelchair-accessible cabins. All American Cruise Lines' other ships have elevator service to all decks. American Cruise Lines will work to cater any dietary needs. Please tell your cruise specialist approximately two weeks prior to your cruise so that they may plan accordingly. Refrigeration is available to store insulin or other medications requiring protection. The ships dock in the heart of each town, so shopping, museums and other points of interest are within walking distance.

Accessible Charter River Cruises

The river cruise options with the *MS Viola* ship consists of two routes; the first through west Germany and the second through the east and south of The Netherlands. The *MS Viola* is fully accessible for people with physical challenges. The luxurious looking and accessible cabins on this ship are unique and what many have been waiting for. The bathrooms are shared but private; it has two doors to two rooms. When a guest from one room is using the bathroom, it's automatically locked for the other room.

The ship consists of the Lower deck, the Main deck, the Panorama deck, and the Sun deck. The Standard rooms are located on the Lower deck and the Accessible rooms on the Main deck. The Panorama deck is where the salon, bar, reading lounge and dining room are situated, as well as the reception, the hairdresser and adapted toilets. The Sundeck can be reached by a spacious elevator. On the Sundeck, you can find a terrace for sun lovers, where you can enjoy a cup of coffee and the constantly changing views. The Sundeck is accessible for all by elevator.

Wheelchairs and mobility scooters are allowed on the ship and can be used at all times. Additional mobility equipment is available on the ship, including electric hoists and shower chairs. The spaces are easily accessible with a wheelchair, as there are no steps or stairs towards these rooms. The spacious sundeck is accessible with a large elevator. The entrance of the ship is wide and has a ramp that's put down at each dock.

14 RENTING MOBILITY EQUIPMENT

No two wheelchair users are alike. As such, no two people with mobility impairments have the exact same combination of accessibility needs. While most cruise lines are generally quite good about accommodating the accessibility needs of passengers, there's no one-size-fits-all solution, and sometimes wheelchair users need assistance that cruise lines can't provide. This is where companies like Special Needs at Sea and Scootaround come in.

Did you know that you can rent an electric scooter just for your cruise, have it delivered directly to your cruise ship cabin before you board, then have it picked up after you disembark? You can do the same thing with other types of mobility equipment as well, such as shower chairs and hoists. But before we get into those details, let's take a look at why renting mobility equipment for a cruise might be a better option than bringing your own.

The most common piece of mobility equipment rented by cruise ship passengers is the electric scooter. It's hard to go on a cruise these days without seeing at least a couple of them parked at the entrance to the theater or dining room, or passengers zipping about while exploring a port of call. Many cruise ship passengers who rent mobility scooters are able to stand and walk shorter distances, but have challenges with standing for longer periods of time or walking longer distances.

It's difficult to overstate how large modern cruise ships can be. If you are a slow walker or require taking lots of breaks, it can take you a long time to get from one end of the ship to another. Many port visits and tours also require a considerable amount of walking, which can be alleviated by the use of an electric scooter. Renting a manual wheelchair can also be extremely helpful to this end. I use a power wheelchair full-time, but I've rented manual wheelchairs before when traveling with my best friend, specifically for ports and shore excursions where manual wheelchairs offer more flexibility with difficult terrain and tour vehicles.

Please keep in mind that while electric scooters can offer more freedom and flexibility in many ways, they can also impose some limitations. Companies who rent them to cruise passengers usually offer a variety of sizes and models. However, if you are staying in a standard cabin, the width of the doorway is usually only 22 inches. The vast majority of scooters won't fit, which means you have two options. You can either reserve an accessible stateroom, which might take it away from a full-time wheelchair user who needs all the accessibility features, or you can disassemble the scooter each time you want to take it in and out of your stateroom, since it's not possible to park it in the hallway for safety reasons.

All this being said, if renting an electric scooter or manual wheelchair will make the difference between you fully enjoying everything about a cruise or being restricted to short distances, I fully encourage you to contact a rental company and find out what your options are. I also highly encourage you to visit one of these mobility stores in person and spend some time practicing on a scooter. Sadly, many renters with poor scooter driving skills have caused museums around the world to prohibit their use due to collisions. Don't give full-time scooter and wheelchair users a bad name by driving around like Mario Andretti after drinking a gallon of espresso.

Other types of equipment that you can rent include rolling shower/commode combination chairs, manual hoists (you have to provide your own sling), small refrigerators, walkers, CPAP machines, and oxygen. Technically, you can even rent adjustable hospital beds from some of these companies, but it will be tougher for you to find a cruise line that will allow you to use one in your stateroom.

The types of mobility equipment that rental companies can offer will vary from embarkation city to city, as will the prices. In addition to these two companies, there are several other mobility equipment rental companies around the world that provide their services locally, particularly for cruises that return to their port of departure. For example, if you are working with a mobility equipment rental company in Barcelona to rent an electric scooter, you may not be able to drop it off in Rome because they have no business partner there who can collect it.

Before deciding if you should rent mobility equipment for a cruise or bring your own, take into consideration what your needs are. If you only need a scooter for long distances and can manage getting to and from the ship before and after the cruise without it, then a rental may be a good idea for you. If you have very specific needs with regards to the shape, size, and function of a power wheelchair, hoist, shower chair, or CPAP machine, then you may want to go through the extra trouble of bringing your own. If you're still not sure what to do, contact your accessible travel agent for assistance, or a mobility equipment rental company that works with cruise lines at your embarkation port.

15 PURCHASING TRAVEL INSURANCE

Flight reservations? Check. Accessible hotel reservations? Check. Travel insurance??? If you're feeling like a deer in headlights when it comes to the need for travel insurance, you're not alone. Many times, we get caught up in the excitement of planning a trip and never stop to think how we would handle certain situations if something goes wrong. For wheelchair users, these odds can be considerably higher if you have a pre-existing medical condition, and we're more likely to get delayed at airports. Read below to learn more about how travel insurance works, the different types of policies you can purchase, and why wheelchair users should never travel without it.

What is travel insurance?

Allianz Global Assistance explains that "travel insurance is designed to cover those who elect coverage with financial safeguards in the case of events ranging from inconveniences to calamities." Coverage may include both costs incurred before your trip, such as nonrefundable event tickets or hotel stays, and during your trip, including travel interruptions and medical expenses. Another element of travel insurance is global assistance. For example, a travel insurance company may offer aid to subscribing travelers ranging from sharing helpful information to arranging for medical evacuations. Some travel insurance providers even have a mobile app where you can file a claim on the spot.

What does travel insurance cover?

This depends on the type of plan you purchase, but most plans will offer reimbursements for things like delayed or cancelled flights, lost or damaged baggage, trip interruption (you have to go home early due to illness or injury), visits to a doctor or emergency room while abroad, and emergency medical evacuation if things get really bad. Levels of reimbursement vary depending on the plan you choose.

When can I use travel insurance?

Generally speaking, most policies won't approve a claim unless it falls under a "covered reason." These often include illness/injury, jury duty, and the death of a family member. They do NOT cover weather events that began before you purchased the policy (such as buying coverage two days after a hurricane started), job-related reasons, and changes of heart. It's extremely important that you read any policies terms and conditions *completely* so you know what will and won't be covered.

Why should I purchase travel insurance?

Simply put? Because stuff happens. Many times, we have to book trips well in advance, particularly with cruises. Do you know what your health situation will be a year from now? If you have an existing medical condition, you can still obtain travel insurance. What if that, or something else, acts up while you're traveling? Odds are your domestic medical insurance policy will NOT cover you in foreign countries.

A fellow travel agent recently posted on social media the stories of two travelers – her client with travel insurance in Jamaica and a gentleman in Mexico without it. Her client got food poisoning and incurred thousands of dollars' worth of medical bills in Jamaica during her recovery. This is all being covered by her travel insurance policy. The second traveler had a heart condition that acted up in Mexico, and he had to be hospitalized and air evacuated to Miami. His family had to start a GoFundMe campaign to raise $30,000 to pay for his hospital bills because he had no policy.

What kinds of travel insurance policies are there?

Generally speaking, there are two main kinds: annual and per-trip. Frequent travelers are well served by an annual policy, which has lower reimbursement rates but covers all their trips for a full year. Infrequent travelers can purchase trip-specific policies, either through an airline to insure flights, cruise lines to insure cruise fares and associated travel booked through the cruise line, or a policy through a travel insurance company based on the overall cost of a trip. You should discuss your plans and needs with an accessible travel agent to make sure you get the policy that best fits in with your plans.

How do I ensure my medical condition is covered?

Not all travel insurance plans cover existing medical conditions, so it's important to discuss your options with an accessible travel agent to make sure you find a policy that does. For travel insurance to cover your pre-existing condition, you must be medically able to travel on the day you purchase your policy. With an existing medical condition, the safest course of action is to get your physician's certification that you're fine to travel before you book your trip. For an existing medical condition to be covered, you must insure your full nonrefundable trip costs. Certain existing medical conditions are excluded from some companies' travel insurance coverage, such as mental and nervous health conditions, bipolar disorder, and Alzheimer's disease.

When should I purchase travel insurance?

It's best to purchase your policy in conjunction with your trip deposit or payment. Third-party companies have a time limit within which you must purchase a policy after you make the first deposit to make sure you're covered for pre-existing medical conditions—usually within fourteen or twenty-one days, depending on the company. Cruise lines let you purchase insurance up to a specific date prior to sailing.

How much does travel insurance cost?

This will depend on how much coverage you want. You can expect premiums to cost somewhere between 5 to 10 percent of your overall trip cost (cruise line policies run around 7 percent of your cruise fare). Generally speaking, the older you are, the higher your premium will be. You should discuss your plans and needs with an accessible travel agent to receive the most accurate policy premium quote.

Should I purchase a policy through the cruise line or a third-party insurance company?

That depends on the components of your trip and your level of risk tolerance. If you purchase a policy through the cruise line, it will cover the full cost of your cruise, as well as any other travel arrangements booked through the cruise line. However, it will not cover pre-existing medical conditions. A third-party policy may not cover the full reimbursement cost of your trip. However, it will cover pre-existing medical conditions (if purchased within fourteen days of your initial deposit), as well as independently booked flights, hotel rooms, etc.

16 FINAL TIPS AND THINGS TO KNOW BEFORE YOUR CRUISE

In my years of cruising as a wheelchair user, I've picked up random bits of valuable knowledge, tips, and tricks for making a cruise easier and more enjoyable. Now, I get to pass those tidbits on to you! Some of these tips may be applicable to you, or none at all. They're just based on my experiences and observations over sixteen cruises as a wheelchair user. I hope they can help!

If it's even remotely possible for your schedule and your budget, make plans to arrive at your departure port city the day before your cruise starts. Airlines are notorious for delays and cancellations, especially during the winter. Don't risk missing your cruise because you cut it too close with flight times!

If you're going to fly home the same day you disembark from your cruise, try not to schedule a return flight before noon. The earliest you can disembark from the ship is typically 7 AM, and that's only if you bring all of your baggage with you. For wheelchair users, this can be challenging. Otherwise, disembarkation times are staggered, and you may not be scheduled to get off the ship until mid-morning. Depending on your disembarkation port location, you may be close to the airport or an hour's drive away (or more). Please keep all of this in mind when booking your return flights.

Don't EVER make the final payment or book flights for a cruise without finding out first if you can get off the ship at most ports of call, or if there are wheelchair accessible things for you to see and do at most ports.

Most cruise lines will let you check in online as early as sixty days before your departure date. Take advantage of this service, and print out all your embarkation forms and luggage tags. This will save you a considerable amount of time during check-in and a luggage drop-off at your departure port.

When you check in online, cruise lines will often let you select your check-in time at the port on your departure date. I would recommend selecting the earliest check in time, which is usually around 12:30 PM, if that works with your schedule. While your stateroom usually won't be ready until around 2 PM, this will give you a chance to board the ship, start getting familiar with the layout before too many people are on board, and eat some lunch before the buffet gets too crazy.

The process of boarding your cruise ship on embarkation day is usually a little crazy. Most passengers typically head straight for the buffet to grab some lunch, and that can get really crowded, especially for a wheelchair user. A little secret is that some cruise ships offer a calm seated lunch in the main dining room on embarkation day. Find out if this is an option for you so you can avoid the buffet insanity.

If you have no choice but to eat at the buffet at any point during your cruise, or if that is your preference, always ask a crew member for help. They will be more than happy to carry your plate for you and put any food on it you want that might be out of your reach. They will also get beverages for you and bring them to your table.

Just because you get your food at the buffet doesn't mean you have to eat there. Part of the reason I don't like the buffet is that the tables are always crowded, especially next to the windows. There's no rule that says you have to eat in the buffet area. I usually take my meal with me on my lap and find a quiet spot to eat next to a large window.

If you have chosen an open dining time (e.g. MyTime, Celebrity Select, etc.), or are cruising on a line like Norwegian that doesn't have scheduled dinner seatings, I highly recommend that you eat very early or very late. If you show up at the main dining room at 7 PM, you could be waiting half an hour or longer for a table.

If you have dietary restrictions, you can often order your dinner a day ahead of time. Each night at dinner in the main dining room, place your order for the following night's dinner with your waiter. Some cruise lines even have separate menus that list additional vegan or gluten-free items.

Be prepared for long waits at the ship's elevators. Especially on cruises with many seniors, you may have to wait a while for there to be enough space in an elevator for you. If everyone is going down at the same time, a good trick is to take an elevator that's going up and then ride it back down. Also, elevators at the very front and back of the ship tend to be less busy than the central bank.

Especially on older ships, you usually won't find too many electrical outlets in your stateroom. If you have electronics or medical equipment that you need to recharge every day, you may want to bring your own extension cord or a power strip. Some cruise lines prohibit these, but will provide one for you upon request.

I know that most wheelchair users don't cruise solo like I do, but you still might want some time in your stateroom to yourself. I always travel with a folding grabber in case something falls out of my reach, like a remote control, or I need to reach a towel, light switch, or the shower head. Even if you're traveling with a companion, it's nice to have some independence when you need to reach something.

Muster drills are a necessary evil for safety before every cruise ship leaves the embarkation port. Sometimes cruise lines will group wheelchair users and slow walkers together. If you have absolutely any questions at all about how you will be evacuated from the ship in case of an emergency, this is the best time to ask. Also, you will usually be released first at the end of the muster drill so you can reach the elevators before the crowd.

If your cruise is sold out, and especially if there are many other wheelchair or scooter users on your cruise, you may want to consider showing up at least fifteen minutes early to theater shows, as well as other popular social events like game shows. The larger the cruise ship, the more reserved spaces will be available for wheelchair users in the theater, but these are limited and available on a first-come, first-served basis.

Just because your ship docks at a port of call doesn't mean that getting on and off the ship will be easy. Most cruise ships make extra space for wheelchair users, and will select the safest gangway. Sometimes you will even go to a gangway separate from all the other passengers. However, tides and weather conditions can still make this quite the adventure. The gangway could be mostly flat when you get off the ship, then inclined at a 30-degree angle when getting back on the ship because of tidal changes. Wet gangways are notorious for being extremely slippery. Make sure you allow the crew to help you board and disembark the ship in your chair as safely as possible.

If you are left alone on a cruise ship in your wheelchair for even ten minutes, or intentionally traveling solo, expect total strangers to approach you and say weird or rude things, or ask weird or rude questions. Typically, people will ask why you're in a wheelchair, or they may ask if they can pray for you. If they see you rolling around the ship by yourself, they may say that you're a good driver, or tell you not to speed, or joke that you shouldn't drink and drive. If you have to back out of an elevator, they'll say you should get something that makes a beeping noise. It's totally up to you how to respond these questions and comments. I just wanted to give you a heads-up that they're quite common on cruises, especially from older Americans.

Many cruise lines have formal dress or gala nights. On shorter cruises, they will only be one night, and on cruises that are seven nights are longer, you will usually have two formal nights. Participating is totally optional. Just keep in mind that some cruise ships don't allow you to eat dinner in the main dining room unless you are dressed up. Some cruises even have theme nights, like pirate night on Disney or the white party on MSC. Check with your cruise line or your travel agent to find out about dress codes or theme nights for your particular itinerary.

On pretty much every cruise ship I have sailed on, the temperature has always been cold on board. Even when it's 90 degrees outside, I usually have a light sweater on indoors. Keep this in mind if you're sensitive to certain temperatures.

If you like massages, facials, or getting your hair done, don't avoid the spa or salon just because you're in a wheelchair. Most modern cruise ships have adjustable treatment tables in the spa, and you can usually stay in your wheelchair to get your hair both washed and styled.

For my final tip, I will start by saying that it is not your job, obligation, or responsibility to represent the entire wheelchair community. Some people are extroverts and some people are introverts. Everybody travels differently. However, if you're up for it, I would highly recommend participating in as many activities onboard as you can. Make new friends at dinner, and join strangers to form a trivia team. Enjoy and soak up every bit of your vacation that is made available to you. Not only does this make life more fun for you; it's one way to help fellow passengers understand that we love to travel just like everyone else, and we deserve to participate in activities like everyone else.

APPENDIX A – TENDER PORTS

I've compiled this list of tender ports from the websites of multiple cruise lines. The ability of a cruise ship to dock or the requirement to tender varies based on the weather, available docking space on a given call date, and docking priority assigned to specific cruise lines. I tried to make this list as comprehensive as possible. However, you should always confirm an itinerary with the cruise line directly or through your travel agent to determine what ports will require tendering. Please note that ports with an asterisk can be either docked or tendered, depending on the call date.

Asia

Benoa (Denpasar), Bali
Halong Bay (Hanoi), Vietnam
Ishigaki, Japan
Jayapura, Indonesia
Jeju (Cheju) City, South Korea
Ko Samui, Thailand
Komodo Island, Indonesia
Lifou, New Caledonia
Malacca, Malaysia
Male, Maldives
Nha Trang, Vietnam
Probolinggo, Java, Indonesia
Sihanoukville, Cambodia*
Uligamu, Maldives

Australia, New Zealand, and South Pacific

Airlie Beach, Queensland, Australia
Akaroa (Christchurch), New Zealand
Alofi, Niue
Alotau, Papua New Guinea
Bahia de' Opunohu, Moorea, French Polynesia
Bay of Islands, New Zealand
Bora Bora, French Polynesia

Cascade, Norfolk Island
Champagne Bay, Espiritu Santo,
Vanuatu
Christmas Island, Australia
Conflict Island, Papua New Guinea
Dravuni Island, Fiji
Easo, Lifou, New Caledonia
Easter Island, Polynesia (Chile)
Eden, New South Wales, Australia
Exmouth, Western Australia, Australia
Fakarava, Tuamotu, French Polynesia
Ghizo Island, Solomon Islands
Gisborne, New Zealand
Gladstone, Queensland, Australia
Hamilton Island, Queensland, Australia
Hiva Oa, French Polynesia
Huahine Iti, French Polynesia
Isle of Pines, New Caledonia
Kaikoura, New Zealand
Kangaroo Island, Australia
Kiriwina Island, Papua New Guinea
Kitava Island, Papua New Guinea
Kuri Bay, Western Australia, Australia
Kuto, Île des Pins, New Caledonia
Mooloolaba, Queensland, Australia
Moorea, French Polynesia
Moreton, Queensland, Australia
Mystery Island, Vanuatu
Nuku Hiva, French Polynesia
Oban (Halfmoon Bay), New Zealand
Phillip Island, Victoria, Australia
Port Arthur, Tasmania, Australia
Port Denerau (Nadi), Fiji
Rabaul, Papua New Guinea
Rangiroa, Tuamotus, French Polynesia
Rarotonga, Cook Islands
Savusavu, Vanua Levi, Fiji
Tabuaeran (Fanning Island), Kiribati
Tadine, Mare, New Caledonia

Tahuata, French Polynesia
Townsville, Queensland, Australia
Vava'u, Tonga
Waitangi (Bay of Islands), New Zealand
Wewak, Papua New Guinea

Caribbean

Basseterre, St. Kitts*
Cap Cana, Dominican Republic
Castries, St. Lucia*
Cienfuegos, Cuba
Cozumel, Mexico*
Devil's Island, French Guiana
Grand Cayman, Cayman Islands
Great Stirrup Cay, Bahamas
Gustavia, St Barthelemy
Half Moon Cay, Bahamas
Princess Cays, Bahamas
Punta Cana, Dominican Republic
Roatan, Honduras*
Saint John, US Virgin Islands
Terre-de-Haut, Guadeloupe

Canada and USA

Charlottetown, Prince Edward Island*
Gaspésie, Quebec
Red Bay, Newfoundland and Labrador
Saguenay, Quebec*
St Anthony, Newfoundland
Sydney, Nova Scotia*

Avalon, California
Bar Harbor, Maine
Catalina Island, California
Gloucester, Massachusetts
Icy Strait Point, Alaska*
Kona, Hawaii Island, Hawaii

Lahaina, Maui, Hawaii
Monterey, California
Newport, Rhode Island
Nome, Alaska
Oak Bluffs, Massachusetts
Santa Barbara, California
Sitka, Alaska*

Europe, Africa, and Middle East

Agadir, Morocco
Alghero, Sardinia, Italy
Alter Do Chao, Portugal
Andalsnes, Norway
Argostóli, Nissos Kefalonia, Greece
Bantry, Ireland
Chania, Greece*
Cannes, France
Cork, Ireland*
Dartmouth, UK
Djúpivogur, Iceland
Dubrovnik, Croatia*
Edinburgh, Scotland
Fishguard, Wales
Flåm, Norway
Geiranger, Norway
Grundarfjordur, Iceland
Guernsey, UK
Heimaey, Iceland
Hellesylt, Norway
Honningsvagt, Norway*
Horta, Azores, Portugal
Ilfracombe, England
Isafjördur, Iceland
Isles of Skye, Scotland
Korcula, Otok Korcula, Croatia
Korsakov, Russia
Kotor, Montenegro
Le Palais, France

Lerwick, Shetland Islands, Scotland
Lüderitz, Namibia
Mamoudzou, Mayotte
Mgarr (Victoria), Malta
Monte Carlo, Monaco
Mykonos, Nisos Mykonos, Greece
Náfplion, Greece
Nanortalik, Greenland
Nosy Be, Madagascar
Ny Alesund, Spitsbergen, Norway
Nynäshamn, Sweden
Paamiut (formerly Frederikshåb),
Greenland
Petropavlovsk, Russia
Plymouth, England
Ponza, Isola di Ponza, Italy
Port Elizabeth, South Africa
Portoferraio, Elba, Italy
Portree, Isle of Skye, Scotland
Qaqortoq, Greenland
Santorini, Greece
Sarandë, Albania
Seydisfjordur, Iceland
South Queensferry (Edinburgh),
Scotland
Split, Croatia*
St Helier, Jersey
St Peter Port, Guernsey
Stornoway, Scotland
Taormina, Italy
Tobermory, Scotland
Trincomalee, Sri Lanka
Ullapool, Scotland
Visby, Sweden
Zanzibar

Latin America

Armação dos Búzios, Brazil

Banana Coast (Trujillo), Peru
Belize City, Belize
Boca De Valeria, Ilha de Tinhare, Brazil
Cabo San Lucas, Baja California Sur, Mexico
Castro, Chile
Fuerte Amador (Panama City), Panama
Gatun Lake, Panama
Golfito, Costa Rica
Icoaraci (Belem), Brazil
Ilhabela, São Sebastião Island, Brazil
Isla Robinson Crusoe, Chile
Loreto, Baja California Sur, Mexico
Parintins, Brazil
Puerto Chacabuco, Chile*
Puerto Montt, Chile*
Punta Arenas, Chile*
Punta del Este, Uruguay
Quepos, Costa Rica
San Blas Islands, Panama
San Juan del Sur, Nicaragua
Stanley, Falkland Islands

* Indicates where a ship can dock or anchor, depending on the cruise line and call date.

APPENDIX B – CRUISE LINE RESOURCES

Because I'm a travel agent, I will always recommend that you book your cruise through someone who specializes in accessible travel. It doesn't cost you anything extra, and you have an advocate on your side who knows how to navigate the booking system to your advantage. However, if you want to contact a cruise line directly while doing your research in order to ask about a ship's accessibility features, here is the contact information for the special needs or accessibility departments of some of the major cruise lines:

Carnival – access@carnival.com / 800-438-6744 ext. 70025

Celebrity – special_needs@celebrity.com / 866-592-7225

Cunard – cunardgroups@cunard.com

Disney – specialservices@disneycruise.com / 407-566-3602

Holland America – halw_access@hollandamerica.com / 800-547-8493

MSC – MSCExistingReservations@msccruisesusa.com / 877-665-4655

NCL – 866-584-9756

Princess – accessofficeprincess@princesscruises.com

Royal Caribbean – special_needs@rccl.com / 866-592-7225

APPENDIX C – WHEELCHAIR ACCESS AT FLORIDA CRUISE PORTS

If you're planning on cruising to the Caribbean, chances are good that you'll be departing from one of Florida's major cruise ports. Hopefully, you've selected a fully accessible itinerary and used an accessible travel agent to help you book an accessible cabin. If so, then all you have to do is show up at your Florida port of departure and sail away! But wait…it's not that simple for wheelchair users. Here are the procedures for requesting wheelchair assistance at the four major Florida cruise ports, what to expect from wheelchair assistance, and the accessible features at each port.

[This information was obtained from the cruise ports' websites, and was current at the time of this publication. Double-check the sites again before you book your cruise.]

Port Canaveral

Port Canaveral is truly a unique place of departure and is Florida's fastest growing cruise port. Located just forty-five miles east of Orlando, visitors can have the ultimate Florida vacation by combining the Orlando theme parks and Space Coast attractions such as Kennedy Space Center with a cruise from Port Canaveral. The cruise terminals are new, innovative and ultra-modern, designed to enhance your overall cruise experience from the moment you enter the terminals until you board your luxury cruise ship. Enjoy a cruise to the Bahamas, Eastern, Western and Southern Caribbean and other tropical destinations or even half-day gaming cruise. Carnival Cruise Line, Disney Cruise Line, Norwegian Cruise Line, and Royal Caribbean International offer a variety of cruises from 3- to 14-day cruises.

Port Canaveral has more recreational facilities than all other Florida Ports combined, including their new Exploration Tower and Cove harbor-side dining and retail area. You also can enjoy Port Canaveral's Jetty Park, which is a 5-acre ocean front beach complete with campground, fishing pier, boat ramps, picnic areas and new refreshment and food concession pavilion. Two other parks are also located at the Port, Freddie Patrick and Rodney S. Ketcham, which are complete with boat ramps, picnic facilities, and viewing areas for manatees and wildlife native to central Florida.

Special Assistance Requests

In order to make sure you have wheelchair assistance waiting for you at Port Canaveral, you need to make arrangements ahead of time with your cruise line. Your accessible travel agent should be able to do this for you, or you can call the numbers below. Please have your reservation number handy!

Carnival Cruise Line: 1-800-438-6744 ext. 70025
Disney Cruise Line: 1-407-566-3602
Norwegian Cruise Line: 1-866-584-9756
Royal Caribbean International: 1-866-592-7225

Each terminal has a limited supply of wheelchairs used to transport guests onto and off the ship, so cruise lines are unable to loan you their wheelchairs for the duration of the cruise. To get wheelchair assistance for boarding the ship, please contact one of the cruise line representatives once you arrive at the cruise terminal and let them know you reserved the service.

Accessible Parking

Port Canaveral no longer offers pre-paid parking. Please pay to park at your cruise terminal's designated parking area and simply take a short walk/roll to your ship's check-in area. Parking is $17.00 per day. Accessible parking spaces are available and the fee is waived for vehicles transporting certain persons who have disabilities that have special equipment, such as ramps, lifts, foot or hand controls for use by a disabled person, display a Florida Toll Exemption Permit as explained in s. 316.1964, Florida Statutes, or display a Florida Disabled Veteran (DV) license plate issued under s. 320.084; s. 320.0842; or s. 320.0845, Florida Statutes.

For passenger safety, security, and convenience, please proceed directly to the cruise terminal to drop off passengers and baggage. Here is where you will request your reserved wheelchair assistance. Porters will assist you with your baggage, and parking personnel will direct drivers to the appropriate parking facility. All parking facilities are convenient, secure and patrolled 24 hours a day. Passenger and luggage drop off is available in front of the terminal or in the parking facility.

Accessible Transfers

If you are cruising on Disney Cruise Lines, they offer accessible transportation for passengers between Orlando International Airport and the cruise terminal, as well as between Disney resorts that are booked as part of a cruise package. If you need an accessible taxi to take you to Port Canaveral from the airport or local hotel, you MUST reserve it ahead of time. Some options include Orlando Wheelchair Transportation and Mears Transportation.

Port Tampa Bay

In close proximity to the top-rated airport in the United States, cruise passengers can take a little more time sightseeing, shopping, and taking in the cultural fare of the city of Tampa. World-class shopping, a unique assortment of museums and top zoos, Busch Gardens, and the allure of Ybor City (the historic Latin Quarter pronounced "EE-bor"), are just a few of the colorful characteristics that make Tampa one of the premier cruise port destinations in the South. Well-appointed luxury hotels and upscale dining are also very close by. Channelside's outdoor plaza is often a venue for live music and provides a perfect setting for socializing and enjoying clear, balmy nights. Adjacent to Channelside, a stop at the Florida Aquarium is essential to those who crave the fascination of the underwater world.

Tampa now homeports five vessels from four cruise lines: Carnival Cruise Lines, Holland America, Royal Caribbean International, and Norwegian Cruise Line, offering the variety of 4-, 5-, 7-, and 14-day cruise itineraries. State-of-the-art in design, the terminals incorporate the far-reaching and diverse needs of all security agencies, while providing a comfortable, expedient cruise experience to customers. Other characteristics of the Port's cruise terminals include customer-friendly information areas, superior security, full passenger amenities and on-terminal parking.

Special Assistance Requests

In order to make sure you have wheelchair assistance waiting for you at Port Tampa Bay, you need to make arrangements ahead of time with your cruise line. Your accessible travel agent should be able to do this for you, or you can call the numbers below. Please have your reservation number handy!

Carnival Cruise Line: 1-800-438-6744 ext. 70025
Holland America Cruise Line: 1-800-547-8493
Norwegian Cruise Line: 1-866-584-9756
Royal Caribbean International: 1-866-592-7225

Each terminal has a limited supply of wheelchairs used to transport guests onto and off the ship, so cruise lines are unable to loan you wheelchairs for the duration of the cruise. To get wheelchair assistance for boarding the ship, please contact one of the cruise line representatives once you arrive at the cruise terminal and let them know you reserved the service.

Accessible Parking

There are three cruise terminals located at Port Tampa Bay. All three are in the same proximity and are all located along the Channel District. The Port Tampa Bay parking garage is located across the street from the central cruise terminal (Port Tampa Bay Cruise Terminal 3 – 815 Channelside Drive, Tampa, Florida 33602). Signs on-site also direct cruise passengers. Parking is free for disabled passengers who have vehicle modifications such as hand controls or ramps. You may also demonstrate 100 percent rated disability with a DMV-issued disabled veteran license plate and/or registration. Accessible parking spaces are available in the garage.

Accessible Transfers

If you need an accessible taxi to take you to Port Tampa Bay from the airport or local hotel, you MUST reserve it ahead of time. Some options include Wheelchair Transport Service and United Cab.

Port Everglades

Port Everglades, located in Greater Fort Lauderdale/Hollywood, Florida, is ranked second among cruise ports worldwide and has more homeported cruise ships than any other port. A common mistake, Port Everglades is not actually part of the wetland ecosystem known as the Florida Everglades. It is located on the southeastern coast of the Florida peninsula within the three cities of Fort Lauderdale, Hollywood, and Dania Beach, as well as unincorporated Broward County. The Port is conveniently situated near the Atlantic Ocean shipping lanes, the Florida East Coast railway, Florida's highway system, Fort Lauderdale-Hollywood International Airport, and the beautiful beaches of Greater Fort Lauderdale and Hollywood. Port Everglades serves all of South Florida and is in close proximity to Miami (twenty-three miles south), West Palm Beach (forty-eight miles north) and Orlando (215 miles north).

Special Assistance Requests

In order to make sure you have wheelchair assistance waiting for you at Port Everglades, you need to make arrangements ahead of time with your cruise line. Your accessible travel agent should be able to do this for you, or you can call the special assistance numbers below. Please have your reservation number handy!

Carnival Cruise Line: 1-800-438-6744 ext. 70025
Disney Cruise Line: 1-407-566-3602
Norwegian Cruise Line: 1-866-584-9756
Royal Caribbean International: 1-866-592-7225
Celebrity Cruises: 1-866-592-7225
Costa Cruises: 1-800-462-6782
Crystal Cruises: 1-310-785-9300
Cunard Cruise Line: 1-800-728-6273
Princess Cruise Lines: 1-800-774-6237
Pearl Seas Cruises: 1-800-981-9146
Silversea Cruises: 1-888-978-4070

Each terminal has a limited supply of wheelchairs used to transport guests onto and off the ship, so cruise lines are unable to loan you their wheelchairs for the duration of the cruise. To get wheelchair assistance for boarding the ship, please contact one of the cruise line representatives once you arrive at the cruise terminal and let them know you reserved the service.

Accessible Parking

There are three entrances into Port Everglades. The 17th Street Causeway entrance which is located at Eisenhower Boulevard, State Road 84 entrance located just off of US 1, and the I-595 East entrance. Proper identification such as a driver's license or passport is required, and your vehicle may be subject to search. Convenient parking for cruise passengers is available in the Northport and Midport Parking Garages and the Northport and Midport Surface Lots. The Northport garage services Northport cruise terminals, including Cruise Terminals 1 and 2. Cruise Terminal 4 has its own dedicated lot with 172 surface parking spaces. The Midport garage services Cruise Terminals 19, 21, 22/24, 25, 26, 27 and 29. Cruise Terminal 18 has its own 600-space surface parking lot adjacent to the term. Port public garages provide disabled parking with unimpeded access to crosswalks and elevators.

In compliance with Florida Statute 316.1964, parking fees are waived at all Port Everglades lots and garages to disabled persons operating vehicles with ONE of the following qualifications: display a Florida Toll Exemption Permit, demonstrate the vehicle is modified with specialized equipment such as ramps, lifts, or foot and hand controls for use by a disabled person, or display the "DV" license plate from any state.

Accessible Transfers

If you need an accessible taxi to take you to Port Everglades from the Fort Lauderdale airport or local hotel, you MUST reserve it ahead of time.

Port Miami

Known worldwide as the "Cruise Capital of the World," PortMiami has been the world's leading cruise port and it continues to advance its No. 1 homeport status with more ships and additional leading-edge passenger terminal facilities. Millions of passengers travel through PortMiami every year, and with twenty-two cruise lines berthing fifty-five ships, PortMiami continues to be the departure destination of choice for cruises to the Bahamas, the Caribbean, Mexico and other exciting destinations.

Special Assistance Requests

In order to make sure you have wheelchair assistance waiting for you at PortMiami, you need to make arrangements ahead of time with your cruise line. Your accessible travel agent should be able to do this for you, or you can call the special assistance numbers below. Please have your reservation number handy!

Carnival Cruise Line: 1-800-438-6744 ext. 70025
Disney Cruise Line: 1-407-566-3602
Norwegian Cruise Line: 1-866-584-9756
Royal Caribbean International: 1-866-592-7225
Celebrity Cruises: 1-866-592-7225
Crystal Cruises: 1-310-785-9300
Azamara Cruises: 1-866-592-7225
Disney Cruise Line: 1-407-566-3602
MSC Cruises: 1-877-665-4655
Oceania Cruises: 1-855-318-2218
Regent Seven Seas Cruises: 1-844-858-4956
Viking Ocean Cruises: 1-855-884-5464

Each terminal has a limited supply of wheelchairs used to transport guests onto and off the ship, so cruise lines are unable to loan you their wheelchairs for the duration of the cruise. To get wheelchair assistance for boarding the ship, please contact one of the cruise line representatives once you arrive at the cruise terminal and let them know you reserved the service.

Accessible Parking

PortMiami is located at 1015 North America Way, Miami, Florida, 33132. Once on-port, follow signs to your destination. Parking is conveniently available at all cruise terminals for $20.00 per day (overnight), or short-term parking (daily) for a flat fee of $7.00. Spaces are also available for over- length vehicles and trailers at special rates. Designated disabled permit parking spaces are available in each garage. All facilities are patrolled by security. Passengers may drop-off luggage at their designated terminal prior to parking; this is where you would request wheelchair assistance from a cruise line employee.

Accessible Transfers

If you are cruising on Disney Cruise Lines, they offer accessible transportation for passengers between Miami International Airport and the cruise terminal, as well as between hotels that are booked as part of a Disney cruise package. If you need an accessible taxi to take you to PortMiami from the airport or local hotel, you MUST reserve it ahead of time.

APPENDIX D – CRUISE SHIP TERMINOLOGY

Aft/forward: The back of the ship is aft and the front of the ship is forward.

Bow/stern: The front part of the ship is called the bow. The back part of the ship is called the stern.

Bridge: The location from which the ship's officers steer and navigate.

Cabin steward: The person who cleans your cabin and turns down the room at night. A steward can assist with minor tasks such as bringing you ice and taking your laundry to be cleaned.

Cruise director: The emcee of the cruise who heads up the entertainment staff and might handle passenger requests and complaints.

Cruisetour: A cruise that is preceded or followed by a bus tour, operated by the cruise line.

Deck: A level or "floor" on a ship.

Disembarkation: Getting of the ship at a port of call or at the end of your cruise.

Embarkation: Boarding the ship at the departure port.

Friends of Bill W/Friends of Dorothy: Friends of Bill W. is the code name for Alcoholics Anonymous meetings on board. Friends of Dorothy denotes LGBTQ+ activities.

Galley: A ship's kitchen.

Gangway: The ramp or stairway that leads from the ship to the pier, allowing passengers and crew members to board and disembark the ship.

MDR: Acronym for main dining room.

Muster drill/muster station: A muster drill is a mandatory event where passengers assemble in a specific location and receive instructions on what to do in an emergency. The muster station is the location passengers must go to during a drill or in an actual emergency.

OBC: On-board credit -- a credit added to your on-board account, either as a perk of booking or as compensation for an unforeseen event.

Port/starboard: The nautical terms for left (port) and right (starboard).

Porthole: A round window, often smaller than the standard picture window found in most outside cabins.

Port of call: A stop or destination during your cruise.

Purser: The officer in charge of financial accounting, who handles billing issues, as well as general customer service.

Specialty dining: A themed dining room typically serving a specific type of food for an additional charge.

Tender: A small boat that ferries cruise passengers from the ship to shore when docking isn't possible.

ABOUT THE AUTHOR

Sylvia Longmire is an accessible travel writer and photographer, travel agent, author, entrepreneur, and disability rights advocate. She is also a service-disabled US Air Force veteran, full-time wheelchair user, single mother, and the former Ms. Wheelchair USA 2016. Sylvia has been on twenty cruises, sixteen of those as a wheelchair user and twelve of those solo.

Ms. Longmire is the founder of the award-winning Spin the Globe travel blog, on which she shares her adventures traveling around the world in a power wheelchair. She focuses on the wheelchair accessibility of her destinations, encouraging fellow wheelchair users to explore the world. Her accessible travel writing has been featured in *The New York Times*, *New Mobility* magazine, *The Orlando Sentinel*, and Lonely Planet, and she has published two travel photography books. Through her travel agency (Spin the Globe/Travel), she is making accessible travel dreams come true for fellow wheelchair users and their families.

Ms. Longmire is also a subject matter expert on Mexico's drug war and border security. She is a frequent guest on major media outlets, providing interviews for CNN, MSBNC, FOX News, NBC Nightly News, and more. Ms. Longmire has been a guest expert on The History Channel's *Brad Meltzer's Decoded* and *America's War on Drugs*, and has also consulted for producers of the National Geographic Channel's *Border Wars* and *Drugs, Inc.* series. She is the author of two books on these issues.

Ms. Longmire is the President and founder of The PreJax Foundation, a 501(c)(3) non-profit that provides scholarships to exceptional students who either have MS or a parent with MS. In December 2019, she was selected as a brand ambassador for *O, The Oprah* Magazine for 2020. She is a single mother to two amazing boys and resides in Central Florida.

FOLLOW SYLVIA LONGMIRE

SPIN THE GLOBE
www.spintheglobe.net

FACEBOOK
Facebook.com/spintheglobeonwheels

INSTAGRAM
Instagram.com/sylvia_longmire

TWITTER
Twitter.com/spin_theglobe

YOUTUBE
Youtube.com/smlongmire